special intentions

To Jeanette -
So nice meeting you -
Enjoy your new blessing!

Laurie Soloman

11/17/11

special intentions
remembering others in personal prayer

Claire Coleman

WestBow
PRESS
A DIVISION OF THOMAS NELSON

All Bible quotations used in Special Intentions are from: The Holy Bible, Today's English Version, New York: American Bible Society, 1993.

WestBow Press books may be ordered through booksellers or by contacting:

WestBow Press
A Division of Thomas Nelson
1663 Liberty Drive
Bloomington, IN 47403
www.westbowpress.com
1-(866) 928-1240

Cover design by Rosemary Tottoroto of PageOne Creative Group.

ISBN: 978-1-4497-2595-2 (sc)
ISBN: 978-1-4497-2596-9 (hc)
ISBN: 978-1-4497-2594-5 (e)

Library of Congress Control Number: 2011917008

Printed in the United States of America

WestBow Press rev. date: 10/7/2011

Advance Praise for
Special Intentions

Special Intentions reminds us of the importance of not simply praying for what we need, but for what others need. Jesus taught us to ask God for our daily bread, but he also asked us to love one another. Commending our friends and families (and co-workers, neighbors, acquaintances and even those who bother us) to the care of God is a key aspect of that love, and an important element of the Christian tradition. Claire Coleman's sensitive new work will help readers to more fully enter into this rich stream of the spiritual life.

—James Martin, author of *My Life with the Saints*

If you've ever said a quick prayer as an ambulance whizzed by or offered up a simple "God help him" at the sight of someone less fortunate, then this book will resonate with your innate sense that prayers have power. Claire Coleman offers a graceful, easy way to benefit others with her beautifully written portraits of those in need. It's not always the ones you know, but those you don't who could use your prayers. Take her advice, say a prayer for a stranger and make the world a better place.

—Patricia Sheridan, Assistant Editor/Features, Pittsburgh Post Gazette

Special Intentions comes from the heart, from a woman who, like Mary, has "kept all these things in her heart." (Luke. 2:19)

This is a book borne of prayer, and at the service of prayer. It is written to help the reader to find words to pray, when words fail, particularly in difficult, often heart-breaking, situations. It is not, though, simply, a book to be read as if reading to God; no, it is a spiritual tool to help us to speak with God, and then to listen to God speaking to us. The author writes from a place of compassion, realizing that when we turn to God in prayer, we bring not only our needs but those of friends, even strangers, to God. Knowing what to say to God often is particularly difficult when we are in unfamiliar territory, asked to pray about something we know little about, or asked to pray for someone we hardly know. Even more difficult is when we are so close to the person in pain that we are speechless, even before God. The author certainly knows that God is not bound to our words, but speaks to us in our silence, and comforts us therein; and, she also knows how to use the written page to create the sacred space that leads to that bountiful silence. While *Special Intentions* is a beautiful meditative book for the person alone in prayer before God; it likely also will be will be an inspiration for those in prayer groups, and friends who come together to talk about their life's journeys. Each meditation is a gentle reminder to "pray without ceasing," specially attentive to the people around us, making their varied intentions our special intentions.

—Dianne M. Traflet, J.D., S.T.D., Associate Dean, Immaculate Conception Seminary School of Theology, Seton Hall University

Prayer is a personal experience, but sometimes we need a little reminder. Claire Coleman's *Special Intentions* is the perfect book to keep close at hand and close to the heart to reference, to inspire, and to share with others.

—Amelia Grey, author of twenty-three books

[The] listings of special intentions are so global and yet personal, so ordinary and yet profound. I can readily imagine their capacity for inspirations that add to these special intentions and also simply invite prayer from those who read the prayer in all kinds of situations and place, prayer that whispers in the heart wherever the "pray-er" is or goes."

—Sr. Joan Noreen, OLME, co-founder and director of Our Lady's Missionaries of the Eucharist

Claire Coleman's *Special Intentions* is a remarkable collection of essays that serve not only as a call to reflection: they are also a call to service. As an alumna of Rosemont College, where we graduate men and women who will be successful ethical leaders devoted to social responsibility, Ms. Coleman reminds us that every one of us is, for very different reasons, in need of prayers. As she points out, most of us do pray, but usually for ourselves or someone we know; her ability to lead us to pray for someone we suddenly notice, think about and then care about—someone who we don't even know—is truly a gift. And those of us who know the power of prayers know that this is indeed great service.

—Dr. Sharon Latchaw Hirsh, president,
Rosemont College, Rosemont, Pennsylvania

For Michael,
Matthew,
Andrew,
and
Maureen

Always in my prayers

Contents

Introduction

"I'll keep you in my thoughts and prayers."

I have written and spoken those words thousands of times. Usually, they were expressed to people dealing with life-challenging moments. Sometimes the words were in condolence letters written upon the death of a parent, spouse, sibling, favorite aunt, or tragically, a child. Other times I said them to someone who was undergoing surgery, healing from an accident, or recuperating from a serious illness. Then, there were times when saying those words to a fearful flyer before a trip, or someone looking for a job or taking the law boards were more like requests for cosmic luck and less like spiritual moments.

Each time I said or wrote those words, I meant it. However, I didn't always follow up diligently with the promised prayers on every occasion. Some things, like my nephew's tour of duty in Iraq and the critically ill grandchild of a friend, stayed embedded in my mind and I offered a prayer—quick, silent, and heartfelt—each time I thought of them. However, there were many other times when the person or circumstances failed to create the mental Post-it for my mind, and I never said the prayers. When I finally did remember, I felt horrible about neglecting the promise and forgetting what was very important to someone else.

On the afternoon of September 11, 2001, I made a list of family and friends who were missing after the terrorist attacks. The list included Richard, my husband's cousin, a passenger on United Flight 93; Frank, a father and husband I had known for years from town; and Michael, another young husband and dad, who worked on one of the upper floors of the north tower of the World Trade Center. There were fourteen names in all. I wrote them down because I knew I needed to pray for each one and I couldn't take the chance of forgetting any one of them. I prayed very hard for each person on that list—that they would be found, that they would survive. By the end of the day, hope had faded for some but not for all. I returned to the list, but, eventually, I learned that not one person on the list survived.

For whatever reason, I couldn't bring myself to tear up the list or throw it out. Instead, I placed it on my night table so I would see it in the morning and before I went to sleep at night. Just seeing that list of names brought to mind all the surviving spouses, children, parents, and siblings of those who were lost. I knew these survivors would carry heartaches and grief for the rest of their lives. I knew I could not change what happened on September 11, and the only thing I felt I had the power to do was pray for the survivors and ask God to comfort those people in their great need. Each time I looked at the list I offered a silent prayer for the families.

In 2004, my brother retired from the Navy after thirty years of active and reserve service. I attended his retirement ceremony, a combination of Navy protocol, traditions, and personal remarks. Near the end of this moving ceremony, an officer read "The Watch," a poem written by William Whiting in 1860.

In part it says:

"He stood the watch so that we,
our families, and our fellow countrymen could sleep soundly in safety,
each and every night,
knowing that a sailor stood the watch."

As soon as I heard these words, I couldn't help but think of the nights that my brother stood the watch on the bridge of his ship and later in the Naval Command Center at the Pentagon. But then, my thoughts went to the thousands of sailors on ships around the world, the scores of people in the Pentagon, the soldiers on active duty in Iraq and Afghanistan, and the men and women of the Air Force, Coast Guard, and the Department of Homeland Security who "stand the watch" every night as I sleep. These people, and so many others, who protect our country, cities, and towns every day and night, deserve my thanks and gratitude. For me, the best way to do so is to offer a prayer for these wonderful men and women.

Curiously, I reacted to September 11 and the retirement ceremony with the same response—I have to say a prayer for those people. Praying for other people is a practice I have embraced as far back as I can remember. I attended Catholic schools for the majority of my academic life and, obviously, praying was a huge part of those experiences. During my senior year of high school, the boy who sat in front of me in my religion class was hospitalized with meningitis. Bruce had one of the greatest happy-go-lucky smiles, and we used to talk about how independent we were with our drivers' licenses, college acceptances, and graduation. From the day after he was taken to the hospital, the morning announcements from the school PA system included an update on his condition and a reminder to keep him in prayer. Sadly, although he survived the meningitis, he died the day before he was to leave the hospital from a pulmonary blood clot. As a school, we then prayed for his family.

When I was growing up, my mother, quietly but consistently, was an example of someone who remembered the needs of other people. For almost twenty years, she helped a woman in town, who had a son late in life and was left without any money when her husband died. The widow was "a little nervous" (my mother's words for anxiety-ridden) and earned some money by taking in laundry and ironing for some of the wealthier families. My mother gave her some of her own clothes—a warm coat, sweaters, and the like while the son received bags of clothes from my brother who seemed to outgrow his clothes as soon as the tags were cut from them. At Thanksgiving and Christmas, we would bring cartons of food to this family. My mother also remembered the poor and needy in prayer; she never failed to follow the recitation of Grace before a meal with the request, "May the Lord provide for the poor and may the souls of the faithful departed, through the mercy of God, rest in peace."

She learned this prayer at her grandmother's table. My siblings and I learned from her example and her ritual to keep the poor in mind and prayer. At any of our family gatherings these days, just try to conclude Grace without that addendum and all the bowed heads pop up as if you announced you forgot to make stuffing or sweet potatoes on Thanksgiving.

From the time they were old enough to recite bedtime prayers, I reminded my children to add someone else to their lists of "God blesses" (God bless Daddy, Mommy, Grammy). Each child brought his or her own thoughtful requests—a classmate with a broken wrist, a friend with a new baby sister, the goalie who cost the team the game. I felt it was important to introduce my children to a depth of prayer as they developed in their faith and their relationship with God.

September 11 and the moving poem at the retirement ceremony, coupled with a personal history of including other intentions in my private prayers, led me to consider writing a book which asked for prayers for people who carry great burdens or who are selfless in their commitments. I believe that praying is a universal act, and a fuller, more developed prayer life involves sincere consideration of the needs of others. The act of reflecting on someone else's life increases our empathy for other people. That reflection may serve to slow our rush to judgments about others; slow our hair-trigger impatience with a waiter, a cashier, or the voice on the other end of the phone. We may, in time, come to realize that no one journeys through life unscathed and that every soul carries some sorrow or sadness. We may come to realize that every one of us could use a caring thought or a dedicated prayer.

At first, when I began writing about those who were to be the inspirations for focused prayers, my pages consisted of a very long list of men, women, and children with various needs. Every branch of the military was mentioned. There was a laundry list of medical situations—people with various cancers, people who are depressed, people who are blind, people who are homeless—but these pages presented a generalized sweeping view of all people with difficult situations.

Then, one day at the special year-end meeting of my garden club, which brings together active and sustaining members of all ages, I watched as one of our more senior members opened the ribbon on a beautifully packaged box lunch and then feed the sandwich, pasta salad, and brownie to another member whose hands were gnarled and contorted with the worst arthritis I had ever seen.

All day long, I thought about that woman with arthritis, knowing that she still lived in her own home. How did she manage on her own? *Did* she manage on her own? What was it like to live like this? How do you adjust from being a person who opened the ground for tulip bulbs, started annuals from tiny seeds, and pruned your own roses to one who is not able to hold your own sandwich? If I was this woman, I would need tremendous strength to open my eyes every morning, much less get up and out to a garden club event.

After that day, I began to realize that reflecting or meditating on a moment in a day of someone with severe arthritis triggered a more emotional response from me than just being aware of the fact that people with arthritis need prayers. Suddenly, I knew it was more important to use *Special Intentions* to describe what one person was experiencing *today* as a way to bring consciousness to situations where a prayer for strength, courage, or gratitude is needed. Therefore, each page of *Special Intentions* is designed to give you someone to think about today—the soldier being fitted for a prosthesis, the parents of a child starting chemotherapy, the elderly man losing his sight and his independence. It enables you to remember people who need strength, comfort, or wisdom or perhaps just a few words of thanks offered in their behalf.

What inspired me to write this book was my belief that many people could and would easily embrace the concept of praying for other people, even people they didn't know. I know that people help other people every day. Instinctively, we grab our phones and call 9-1-1 to report a fire or a car accident. We sign up by the thousands to walk for breast cancer, juvenile diabetes, and Alzheimer's. We send money to the Red Cross for victims of floods, tornadoes, and earthquakes. If you are a person with that instinct to help, with that concern for others, and with that empathic heart, it is easy to take those qualities and combine it with a prayer. Then, after calling 9-1-1 to report a fire, you say a prayer for the family whose home is being destroyed by the fire. After you "walk for the cure," you meditate on the life of one woman whose life is changed today when she is diagnosed with cancer.

Think of *Special Intentions* as a book of reminders to continue your sense of caring for others into the realm of prayer. It is like the string around your finger, the rubber band on your wrist, or the shocking pink Post-it note on your bathroom mirror. When you read a page, you are reminded to do something important, as each page presents the reader with an individual meditation for a prayer. The concept behind *Special Intentions* is simple:

Say one prayer,
every day,
for someone other than yourself.

I suggest that you select only one page each time you open *Special Intentions*. You can begin with the first page or with a random page. Select a reading that speaks to you and take time to quietly reflect on the words and the life it describes. Then, offer a prayer. The deeper you meditate on the life described, the easier the words of prayer will flow from your heart. Your initial emotional response to the "person" on the page is your first prayer. The most fervent prayer rises from the most sensitive place in your heart. It is empathy. It is compassion. It is gratitude.

While *Special Intentions* acknowledges the great need for prayers, it also acknowledges that prayer and perseverance go hand-in-hand. For example, a seriously obese man, despondent over his situation, could also be the focus of continued prayer for strength and self-love. A single parent, who has few days in the year that are stress-free or uncomplicated, could benefit from your daily prayer. Maybe your prayer will help him or her through a particularly difficult day. If you find a page in the book that resonates with you and you want to remain for a few days on that page, do so. If this were a "prayer-a-day" book, there would be 365 pages. You are the one who decides for whom you want to pray and for how long.

Although written for readers who pray regularly and believe in prayer as central to their faith, this book can be used easily by anyone who has never prayed in this way before. All that is required is an interest in adding this dimension to your prayer life and a willingness to devote time to it. It also is a great book for people involved in prayer groups or prayer circles, who combine their voices and commit to the power of communal prayer. You can literally be on "the same page" with a group, praying for the same person. There is no right or wrong way to use *Special Intentions* as a means to enhance your prayer life. It can be used if you pray once a day, once a week, or once in awhile.

One small thing to note with the type of prayer suggested in *Special Intentions*: There is no instant gratification or maybe even long-term gratification, because, for the most part, your prayers will be offered for a stranger—a member of the Coast Guard, a nurse in a burn unit, a single father. The important thing to note is that intercessory prayer, as it called, is a selfless act rooted in the belief in the power of prayer, the trust that your prayer truly will be heard, and the love of God for all God's people.

There are no books exactly like *Special Intentions*. There are many books about prayer that focus on your own problems and needs. This is a book that asks you to read about one person, reflect on his or her life, and offer a silent, heartfelt prayer for the needs of that person. It is a book that will help you in your journey towards a more fully developed prayer life, one that is aware and sympathetic to the needs of others. I sincerely hope you find a personal connection to *Special Intentions*.

I have included blank pages in the back of the book for you to enter the special intentions that you would like to keep in your thoughts and prayers.

Claire Coleman
February 2011

Chapter 1

Love One Another

"And so the Father will give you
whatever you ask of him in my name—
this, then, is what I command you:
love one another."
(John 15:16–17)

Across the Aisle

Look across the aisle,
a movie aisle,
the bus aisle,
the church aisle,
any aisle,
and say a short prayer for someone you see.
Maybe you know his name, maybe you don't.
Maybe you know her sorrows, maybe you don't.
Maybe she looks as though she doesn't have any.
She does. He does.
We all do.
So say a private prayer for someone—
so he or she may receive the spiritual support,
the grace, or the wisdom needed for the issues he or she faces.

The Black Sheep of the Family

They are the black sheep, the renegades, the screw-ups,
the contrary ones, the turncoats, the bad eggs.
Sometimes they lose the label as they get older,
and the term is said with affection as they outgrow
what makes them different from the rest of the family,
or the family actually embraces those differences.
But for others, there is little affection for the child
who has taken his or her own path,
the artist among a family of scientists,
the rock musician among a family of classical pianists,
the motorcycle mechanic from a family of bankers and lawyers.
Sometimes, the life of the contrary one involves drug or alcohol abuse,
and the estrangement from the family is deep.
Say a prayer today for the black sheep of the family
and for understanding within families,
so that all black sheep remain lovingly within the fold.

The Soup Line

Every day, men and women file in to churches and shelters
for the hot meals being served there.
Not everyone taking the meal is homeless.
Sometimes it is a migrant worker who, without this meal,
has no meal today.
Sometimes it is an elderly person who lives alone,
and eating with strangers once in a while
is better than eating alone every day.
Other times, it is a maintenance worker from a nearby building
who needs to save money for his family
and humbles himself to stand in line for a free meal.
Maybe it's a young welfare mother
who uses this as a way to feed her children
without spending what little money she has.
There are no judgments handed out along with the food.
Just a prayer today that those on the soup line
receive the nourishment they need.

Morning People

There are people who make bagels or bake bread,
serve us coffee or scrambled eggs in the diner,
deliver or sell the newspapers, drive the school bus,
crew the early train or the first plane out,
open the gas station,
stock the supermarket shelves or raise the flag in front of the building.
No matter what issues are going on in their lives,
big or small,
they show up.
They are the caretakers for the rest of us
who can't start the day without caffeine,
the sports or business section of the paper,
the early flight, early bus, or early train.
Say a prayer of gratitude.

Family Ties

There are lots of jokes about grandparents who spoil grandchildren.
Some grandparents would love the opportunity to spoil someone,
but either because of divorce or distance,
they rarely see their family.
Occasionally they do,
but there is no familiarity, no long hugs, no nicknames, no laughter.
Only awkwardness.
Say a prayer today for a family like this.
Pray that someone takes a first step
toward breaking down the barriers that exist
so that they can begin to know each other
and experience joy in each other's company.

Over There

There are people of all ages who leave their homes and families
to volunteer with international agencies.
Sometimes they build houses, roads, or water and sewer systems.
Sometimes they teach English, reading, math, or science.
Sometimes they immunize and vaccinate, perform surgery, set bones,
diagnose illnesses and diseases, deliver and save high-risk babies.
Sometimes they comfort the displaced refugee,
the raped woman, the orphaned child.
Sometimes they get discouraged
because there is always so much work to do.
For the volunteer who leaves the comforts of home
to help others who have so little,
say a prayer of gratitude and support
for their selfless service.

The Immigrant

We are a country of immigrants.
Few among us can claim ancestors in this country
from a time before Columbus.
However, with so many people coming into our country illegally,
the word now carries a negative connotation.
Not all immigrants are here illegally.
There are legal immigrants who work hard—
studying at universities, logging hours as office workers,
painting houses, laying bricks, landscaping buildings,
cleaning offices, serving fast food—
often doing backbreaking work or jobs that no one else would do.
Many live from paycheck to paycheck,
have no health insurance
and try to assimilate into a fast-paced culture.
They have come to America for a better life
for themselves and their children.
They are willing to work long hours at difficult jobs to do so.
In the meantime,
say a prayer today for the immigrant who struggles for a better life
through work and love of this country.

Homeless

The cities have hundreds of them, maybe even thousands.
Small villages and towns might have one.
A homeless person.
Reasons why she is homeless vary greatly but the fact is
she lives someplace other than a house.
Maybe in a subway tunnel in New York City,
maybe under a bridge in Chicago,
maybe in an abandoned building in Topeka,
but it is not a home.
Think about the twenty-four-hour routine of a person with no home
and pray that tonight he or she is safe,
and sheltered from the elements.
Pray, also, that those who look to change their plight
have an opportunity to do so.

Claire Coleman

In the News

Listen to the news today and pray for one person
who made one of the stories.
Maybe it was the secretary of state
flying to another country on a peace mission,
or maybe the mayor of a city or town dealing with a crisis,
or someone involved in a multi-car pile-up on the freeway
or a local team going to a state championship.
Just say a prayer for someone else as he or she goes through the day.

Relocated

How strange it is to spend an entire day in your town
and not see a familiar face
or anyone who can greet you by name.
For someone who has relocated to another city,
town, or the other side of the country,
this is what the first few days or weeks are like.
They need maps to find the grocery store,
the gas station, and the movie theater
and then get lost trying to get back home.
Maybe today, with a prayer from you,
the family known as the "new people on the block"
will be recognized or acknowledged by a new neighbor or a shop owner
and feel just a little more at home.

Family Reunions

Some families live close enough to spend holidays together,
others have to travel great distances to be together.
Some families gather all parts of an extended family at reunions,
which take months to organize.
Multi-generations meet and get re-acquainted,
strengthen the connections between parents, siblings, cousins,
aunts and uncles, and in-laws.
It can be a time of great joy
or an opportunity for family feuds to re-appear.
For one family who has come together out of love for one another,
say a prayer that old grudges are forgiven and forgotten
and that family bonds are intensified.

Every Single One

Even the most charmed life
will reveal sorrow and pain when closely examined.
Every single person you pass today,
on the street, in a store,
at work, at a restaurant,
at the gym, in the park,
in the market,
carries some pain, some issue, some burden,
some regret, some sense of distress or anguish
that could emotionally buckle his or her knees
at any point in the day.
It is always there,
every day,
in each one of us.
Today, say a prayer for someone else
so that he or she receives what is needed to deal with what they face.

Chapter 2

Carry the Burdens

"Carry each other's burdens,
and in this way
you will fulfill the law of Christ."
(Galatians 6:2)

Feeding the Very, Very Hungry

There are men, women and children who are starving to death.
Maybe there are some in your town or state.
For certain, there are thousands dying in countries
where poverty levels are high,
or where the government refuses to accept relief donations,
or where a natural catastrophe has made roads impossible to use.
Men, women, and children will die if food is not received soon.

Please, say a prayer today that food and water reach those in great need
and those who may not make it to the end of the week.

Whirlwind

Three weeks after a tornado ripped through their home,
a family still needs prayers.
After the tragedy, desperately needed help arrived
from people in neighboring cities and towns.
Volunteers offered food, clothing, and places to stay.
Pieces of their house remain scattered over acres of land,
and they are working hard to put their life back together.
Insurance claims and government relief paperwork
require documentation,
But the documents of their lives
were stolen by the storm.

Today, remember this family with a prayer
so that they receive support, comfort and guidance
as they make their way through this maze of shock and disbelief.
Ask that hope be restored to them.

Bullied

Somewhere, today, a kid will be bullied.
He knows it will happen
because it happened yesterday
and the day before that.
Today will be no different.
He wishes he could be invisible in school,
and he does everything he can to be small, unnoticed,
or to disappear from the sight of others.
Unfortunately, it is his spirit that is shrinking
and his self-image that is fading.

Please say a prayer for the bullied child today,
so that he does not disappear from everyone's sight.

A Teen Mom

Say a prayer today for the teenage girl who is pregnant.
Pray that she receives the support, guidance, and love
that she needs at this time,
as well as medical care for her health
and that of the baby she carries.

Your prayer for this girl can be prayed for nine months,
because each day will bring this young mother new challenges.

The Smallest Addict

The baby born with AIDS or a drug addiction
is the saddest victim of all.
The tiny body is at war with itself from the first breath.
He will require special care, endless patience,
unconditional love, and specific knowledge of his needs.

This little baby will need so many prayers during his life.
Start with one today,
so that he can endure the struggles ahead
and thrive in a loving home.

Car Habitants

Secrets are hard to keep
and right now, there is a family desperately protecting their secret.
For months they have been sleeping in their car.
After the apartment fire, they stayed with friends,
but that reached its limits.
It is hard to find a place to live in the city,
when the money needed upfront for rent and security just isn't available.
But their car was available, and that's where they huddled one night,
never thinking it would be anything longer than one night.
But it has been weeks.
They return from work and school to the shame of the car.

Today, first pray that this family finds a home,
just a few rooms to live in
which will renew their spirit
and dissolve the secret and shame they carry.
Secondly, pray more people realize that sometimes,
circumstances beyond anyone's control
force people to live in ways they could never imagine
and no one should pass judgment.

1 in 800

Statistically, 1 baby in 800 births is born with Down syndrome.
For the parents presented with this news about their baby,
life takes a huge detour from the script they saw for their lives.
It is normal to be overwhelmed by emotions,
but with loving support from family and friends,
these parents will find their way.

Please say a prayer for the parents
of that special 1-in-800 baby
who comes into the world today.

The Last One

It is hard to be the last one to survive.
The spouse, the siblings, the rest of the family,
and even close friends are gone,
or live so far away they might as well be.
The last one.
The last one who remembers
the family, the home, the finer times.
The last one who can tell stories
about childhood, summer vacations,
or holidays from years ago.
There is no one who answers with a nod of the head
or a smile that says, "I remember that, too."

Today pray for the last one standing
that he or she makes a connection with someone
and has a chance to reminisce again.

The Advocate

There is money in the school system for kids like her young son.
He has Asperger's syndrome, a form of autism, and very special needs.
At six, he is smart enough to know
the names of planets and constellations
but he will not be able to learn math
like the other twenty kids in the class.
He is smart enough to learn,
but needs help to unlock the chambers in his brain
and open the world to him.
Special teachers, special instruction, special attention in some subjects.
His mother knows she has to be her boy's educational advocate.
The job of researching what is needed,
consulting with occupational therapists, medical professionals,
special education teachers, and school supervisors
falls mostly on her shoulders.
It is deeply fatiguing, but he is her son and so she fights on for him.

Say a prayer for this mom today,
that even if she bends from the stress of this situation,
she never breaks from it.

Demons

Maybe it's pills,
maybe it's alcohol,
maybe it's food,
maybe it's pornography,
maybe it's spending money,
but today someone is battling his addiction demon.
Maybe he has had professional help for it
and is now living one day at a time, trying to stay the course.
Maybe he has never gotten help
and believes he can stop his destructive behavior on his own.
This is a day to bring spiritual support to someone
who is in a fight for his life.

Wildfires

Every year wildfires rake through communities
in this country and other countries.
The speed and unpredictability of the fire is astounding.
The devastation left in its path is beyond comprehension.
The people who return to their homes often find nothing
but charred remains of the things they owned.
Furniture, books, photographs, papers, memories reduced to ash.
Today, or some other day, when you hear of fires raging
across acres of homes,
say a prayer for the family who must rise from the ashes.

Children from Divorced Families

Children who grow up in divorced families have scars.
Sometimes, it is because they have lived through,
and remember, the terrible fights between their parents.
Maybe they were asked to take sides in the arguments
or forced to chose one parent over the other.
Maybe guilt is the scar they carry
because they feel like they were the reason for the divorce,
or because they are happy to be in a home without fighting and abuse.
There is a range of emotions,
a flip-flopping visitation schedule,
and a damaged view of marriage as a workable partnership.

A child from a divorced family carries thoughts, worries, and concerns
which may or may not be voiced.
Pray that the child has a safe listener
and wise counsel in someone close to her,
who can help her weather the years.

Pawns

Divorce is bad enough for children to live through
but when one parent physically abducts a child,
it is, in essence, kidnapping.
Not only has the child become a pawn in an adult conflict
but the psychological and emotional effects
of being held against your will and forbidden to return home
are enormous and long lasting.
Statistically, the majority of children are abducted by the divorced father
and they almost immediately leave the state,
some try to leave the county.
With the help of missing children bureaus, some children are returned.
Many cases remain open for years.

For the child who has been abducted by a parent,
say a prayer for the fear, the anxiety, the sorrow he or she carries.
For the parent who waits for news that will locate an abducted child,
say a prayer for the fear, the anxiety, and the sorrow he or she carries.

Per Chance to Dream

In countries where guerilla warring factions haunt days and nights
with killings, rapes, and kidnappings,
how can a person sleep soundly?
How do you sleep when each night could bring terror and death?

Today, say a prayer for one of these brutalized families
in one of these vulnerable villages.
A prayer that they are protected from harm,
free from fears and anxieties long enough
to close their eyes and deeply rest
from the hell that surrounds them.

Aging

Someone is trying desperately to hold on to life as she has lived it.
But, time seems to be moving fast,
and age is robbing her of health and independence.
She wants to remain in her home, drive her car, and cook for herself,
but her family wants her to live in a community of elderly people
who depend on others for meals,
their laundry, a ride to the store, a visit with a friend.
She always did those things for herself
and has managed to do them
long after many women her age had to stop.
For years, her family applauded her for her independence.
Now their plans could strip her of it.

Say a prayer today for this woman and her family—
that her need to remain independent is recognized and respected
as long as it does not jeopardize her health or safety.

Fighting Mad

Parents want their children to stay away from drugs.
They tell them, in no uncertain terms,
that drugs are lethal.
If drugs don't kill your body,
they kill your spirit, your soul,
your dreams, your chances.
But drugs are out there
in schools, neighborhoods, cities and towns.
There are people, classmates, friends, and teammates
who are okay with drugs
and they have no problem saying so.
They contradict *everything* parents say.
Sometimes those people spend more hours with the vulnerable child than
the parents.

For the parent who is waging a war of words over drugs,
who lives in the battle zone and on the frontline of the war,
say a prayer for perseverance,
courage, and the right words at the right time
for this parent to be a strong force
against the corrupting influence of drugs.

Just the Two of Us

After the doctor and nurse leave the room, a parent and child remain.
The little one is tethered to an IV line for chemotherapy
and the other, with a pained heart, stays as support.
Watching a child endure the rigors of cancer treatment
is one of the hardest tests parents must go through.
There is no way to take the burden from the child,
there is no pill or potion they can create as a cure,
there is only patience, strength, compassion, and love to see it through.

In many places today,
a mom or a dad sits by a son or a daughter holding hands,
reading a book,
or watching a DVD together
and, all the while, prays
that the chemicals circulating in the child's body
erase the nightmare
and life returns as it was before.
Add your prayer to theirs.

BFF

She is the best friend you hardly know anymore.
You were always so close,
but now there is so much that weighs her down:
a workaholic husband,
an elderly father with severe medical needs,
three busy kids moving in three different directions,
and a less-than flexible job.
She goes through her day with a checklist of errands and obligations
that a staff of five couldn't handle.
She doesn't laugh as much and, for the first time,
your beautiful, happy friend is angry at life and cries easily.
She thinks she has to handle it all.

Today say a prayer for the friend who needs it the most.

Self-Intervention

Today, someone is on the brink of admitting he has a drinking problem.
No one is forcing him to do it.
It has been a feeling in the pit of his stomach for months.
He likes to drink,
he likes the way it tastes,
he likes the way it makes him feel,
he likes what it lets him forget.
Lately, he has not liked what drinking is doing to his body,
his health, his friendships, his career.
It may be time to stop.
But he doesn't know if he can give up drinking
for the rest of his life.

Maybe with a few prayers
he will find the strength to ask for help with his drinking.
Say that prayer.

Chapter 3

No Greater Love

"Greater love has no man than this,
than to lay down one's life for his friends."
(John 15:13)

Happy Birthday, Soldier

It is a soldier's birthday today,
and he is seven thousand miles from home.
There is a little celebration
and a lot of pats on the back from his buddies,
but he is trying to push away the images of birthdays at home
with his mom's chocolate cake and his family at the table.
His mother has her own thoughts she keeps at bay,
like the fact that twenty-two years ago
she gave birth to an eight-pound baby boy
who is now an army lieutenant leading a platoon in a desert country.
It is not what she imaged when she held him in her arms the first time.

Pray that on his twenty-third birthday this soldier, this son,
will be home,
safe and sound,
and eating chocolate cake with his family.

The Soldier

War is hell,
yet our soldiers are sent into it when ordered to do so.
The men and women who serve in the army
are stationed around the world, many in harm's way every day.
Sometimes their living conditions are the hottest,
the coldest,
the wettest,
or the snowiest
but they dig in and stand at the ready.
Their commitment to this country supersedes
their personal wants and needs.
They train for months, sometimes years, to be the best and strongest.
Our deepest, thankful prayer for the soldiers of the U.S. Army.

A Veteran

No one can imagine the scenes of war if he or she has not been there.
We see pictures and movies,
but the soldier who witnessed D-Day,
the scenes behind the gates of concentration camps,
napalm burns, missing limbs, children caught in the crossfire,
and the work of suicide bombers in Iraq,
holds details and images in his or her heart and psyche
that probably can never be fully described.
Some things he or she shares, some things he or she never will.

For a veteran of any war—
say a prayer of thanks
for stepping forward when called
and a prayer that somehow, some way,
he handles the horrors of war he cannot forget.

For Those Who Served

There are men and women in veterans' hospitals
in every state in the union.
They receive medical care
for having worn the uniform and served our country.
It doesn't matter whether they were a major, a captain, or a cook;
there is a bed waiting and staff ready to care.
Say a prayer today for someone in a veterans' hospital,
may he or she receive quality care with our thanks.

In the Navy

Say a prayer today for someone in the Navy.
Someone on an aircraft carrier or a naval base far from home
and charged with the task of protecting this country.
Whether he or she is the ship's cook or captain,
office clerk, or intelligence officer,
this person is working for us and our freedom.

Your prayer today will be a spiritual sign of support and thanks.

Serving in the Marines

They storm beaches.
They walk foot patrols.
They lead the way for other forces.
They conduct their lives according to a code of honor.
They are our young men and women who serve in the Marine Corps.

Say a prayer of thanks for the few, the proud, the Marines.

Casualty of War

Victims of Agent Orange from the Vietnam War
were dismissed as delusional or as hypochondriacs.
Finally, medical evidence proved their case and they were validated.
Each day, they live with the horrible health effects of the chemicals.

Please add a victim of Agent Orange to your prayers today.

Men and Women of the National Guard

When they signed up for the National Guard,
they never thought they would be standing in a sand storm in Iraq,
or the mountains of Afghanistan,
but it happened.
The wars have dragged on for years longer than anyone expected,
and the National Guard has been asked to step into situations
they never expected.

For the men and women of the National Guard
deployed around the world,
say a prayer of thanks
and a prayer for their safe return.

Claire Coleman

The Mommy Soldier

Placed among our fighting troops
in countries far from home is a soldier serving our nation.
She may be called private, specialist, corporal, or captain
but she is just Mommy to the two little girls who wait for her.

Offer a prayer today for one soldier's safety while deployed
and offer another prayer for the children
who want their mom to come home.

US Coast Guard

Men and women who serve in the US Coast Guard take an oath
to protect the people of this country,
the environment, and the economic interests
of the US in ports and waterways along the coast,
and in international waters.
They rescue people in distress on the water,
respond to oil and chemical spills,
examine vessels coming into our ports,
inspect waterfront facilities,
as well as perform a critical role
in homeland security
and the war against illegal drugs coming into this country.

Say a prayer of thanks for those who serve in the US Coast Guard.

From Sea to Shining Sea

They identify native plants and invasive plants.
They set controls for hunting and fishing to protect the animals.
Whether it is the preservation of a small alpine flower,
the creation of a trail through a natural wildlife preserve,
or protecting the bald eagle from extinction or hunting,
the men and women of the US Fish and Wildlife Service
work for the American people.
They protect wetlands, forests, deserts,
and the animals that live there.
They arrest coral smugglers, poachers,
and those who pollute the environment.
They insure that certain species of trees are not forested out of existence,
that rivers and streams remain clean,
so that the abundance of native American fish flourish.
They have designed one thousand trails in our national parks,
just for us.
The physical territory and numerous areas of responsibility
that fall within the mission
of the US Fish and Wildlife Service is staggering.
Say a prayer of thanks for the enormously important work they do
to maintain America the beautiful.

The Brave

We ask firefighters and police forces in cities and towns,
soldiers and sailors stationed home and abroad,
security personnel and first responders of every nature
to be courageous for us.
We ask them to pull us from a burning building or a mangled car.
We ask them to protect us from a mugger, a car thief, a terrorist.
We ask them to run into situations everyone else is running from.
We ask them to be courageous every minute of every day.

A prayer of thanks, today, for those who have chosen
to be courageous for us.
Pray that God will keep them safe
and protect them while they are protecting us.

Chapter 4

With Thanks

"I thank God every time I remember you."
(Philippians 1:3)

Standing the Watch

While you sleep, someone stands the watch.
He is the security guard at the office, the police officer,
or the firefighter on the nightshift.
She works in the Pentagon
or the emergency room, or as a 9-1-1 dispatcher.
Other people, in airports around the country,
carefully watch fleets of planes
which will transport thousands of people tomorrow.

Say a prayer for wakefulness and stamina.
Say a prayer of thanks for those who are doing their jobs
while you rest from yours.
They stand the watch for all of us.

Coffee and Donuts

Volunteers from the Red Cross serve up more than coffee and donuts.
They open shelters for those evacuated from their homes,
or for those suddenly without homes.
They serve hot meals and, when needed,
bring in medical and mental health professionals.
They conduct blood drives in every state in the nation.
When the worst strikes day or night,
they mobilize and come prepared to ease the pain and burdens.

Say a prayer of thanks for the Red Cross volunteer
who is ready to help today and every day.

Operation Smile

Dentists and medical support teams make a difference
in children's lives when they volunteer for Operation Smile.
These professionals travel thousands of miles and use their skills
to help children without access to dental care.
In some cases, doctors reconstruct a small face
deformed by a cleft palate or harelip,
and give the child a chance for a more normal life.
All because someone cared.

The people of Operation Smile deserve a prayer of thanks.

Tutors

Say a prayer of thanks for people
who tutor children with learning disabilities.
They relentlessly chip away at neurological roadblocks
which make reading, writing, spatial relations,
and fine motor skills very difficult for some kids.
There isn't much fame or fortune for these tutors,
but being part of a child's breakthrough moment is priceless.

Habitat for Humanity

From coast to coast, houses are being built,
families are moving into homes,
and communities are being revived and restored.
All because someone picked up a hammer, a paintbrush, or a putty knife.
The Habitat for Humanity volunteers foster this phenomenon.
Whether they volunteer for one project or twenty,
they renew the landscape of this country.

Say a prayer of thanks for the person who wielded a nail gun
or pushed a broom, so a house could become a reality.

Patchwork

There are many hands measuring and cutting fabric,
guiding it under needles of sewing machines,
pressing seams, and adding final touches to quilts
for children battling cancer.
The quilts are for the children when they receive chemotherapy,
cope with its after effects,
endure pain,
and mourn days of missed childhood.

Say a prayer of thanks for all who create quilts
that will be held by small hands.

Night Vigils

Last night someone sat in the emergency room next to a dying friend.
There was no one else to hold her hand,
raise a cup of water to her lips,
adjust the blanket over her shoulders,
or watch her breathing as she slept.
This good friend stayed all through the night
until the inevitable occurred.

Say a prayer of thanks for all those friends
who give of themselves at desperate times.

Hospice Professional

Today, say a prayer of thanks for those who work in hospice care.
Their tenderness and understanding of the final days of life
ease physical and emotional pain for the dying and the surviving.
Their skills are remarkable gifts and for that, we should be very grateful.

Claire Coleman

Caregivers

In nursing homes, assisted living residences, and private homes,
there are men and women who care for the elderly.
They feed, bathe, and dress those who no longer can care for themselves.
They administer medications,
they dress wounds and bedsores,
they push wheelchairs,
they walk alongside the person with a walker,
they help with physical and speech therapy.
They speak with compassion
to the anxious,
the confused,
and those with severe dementia.
Say a prayer of thanks today for the caregivers,
they are gifts to the aged and infirmed.

Friends with Flowers

A group of volunteers meet once or twice a week.
Some bring flowers, some vases,
and some simply come to arrange.
They create small floral arrangements
which are sent to care facilities,
to patients who never receive flowers.
The volunteers do not sign their names to any cards or stickers,
there is no form of identification of the donors,
except, "Friends with Flowers."

How wonderful to remember those who may be forgotten by others!
How kind to send a small bedside bouquet of bright fresh flowers
and include only a message of love.
Thank you, Friends, we say a prayer for you today
and those you may inspire by your acts.

The Good Earth

From Maine to California, and beyond to Alaska and Hawaii,
farms exist in every state.
Some are very big and managed by corporations.
Others are small—family-owned and operated.

Offer a prayer for the farmer who continues the process
of sowing and harvesting,
season after season,
who often finds a hostile partner in Mother Nature,
but nonetheless, returns to the fields each year.
Honor this testament to his faith in the land,
his commitment and dedication to the farming tradition,
and his perseverance and struggle in such a physically demanding job.

Foster Parents

Foster parents become foster parents for many different reasons.
They are big-hearted people who take on the role
as parents to children in need
and provide love and guidance
to children whose parents are unable to do so.
Say a prayer of immense gratitude for a foster parent.

Claire Coleman

Willing to Adopt

At some point, the decision to adopt is made.
Perhaps, it is by a couple who can't have their own child,
perhaps, by a gay couple,
or perhaps, a single person.
All are willing to take the responsibility for a child,
and love and raise the child as their own.

Say a prayer of thanks for those who make the decision to adopt
and make a huge difference in a child's reality.

Public Defenders

"You have a right to an attorney . . .
if you cannot afford an attorney, one will be appointed for you."
Who are these attorneys who do not select their clients?
They are men and women who believe in our legal system so much
they choose to work in the public defender's office
and be appointed to cases.
If it weren't for these attorneys, the justice we treasure would fail.

Today, say a prayer of thanks
for the men and women who validate our Constitution
and defend people who cannot afford to pay for legal services.

Nature Lover

Neatly manicured gardens,
greenhouses filled with hundreds of plants in bloom,
and beautifully landscaped parks
are the products of people
who don't mind dirt beneath their fingernails
or grass stains on their clothes.
The same people allow us to buy tulips in winter,
synchronize bright blooming poinsettia plants with Christmas,
advise us on our garden plans,
and answer our questions about crabgrass and bugs on our roses.
Just say a prayer of thanks for a nature lover
who makes the world a prettier place.

RN

Nurses, nurses, nurses everywhere—
in the ER, the OR, the pediatrician's office,
the cardio unit, the geriatric wing, the recovery room.
Some are as specialized as the doctors they assist.
They are a vital link between patient and physician.
Very often, they spend more time with the patient
and listen longer than the doctor.

Say a prayer of thanks for nurses who embrace their jobs with compassion.

A Bit of Themselves

Some who donate to blood drives
show up and answer the call on a regular basis.
Others donate once in a while.
They all recognize the need for blood in our health care system,
for emergencies and non-emergencies.
All are willing to take the time to give.
For those who have given gallons or just a pint,
Say a prayer of thanks for their gift.

Treating the Burned

The doctors and nurses who dedicate the work
of their hands and hearts to burn victims
deserve a prayer today.
Not everyone could see what they see,
touch what they touch,
smell what they smell,
and compassionately focus on the science of treatment.

Mentors

Men and women who volunteer to coach children
give of their time and knowledge to instruct and guide.
Say a prayer of thanks for those busy people
who always seem to find the time
to lend a hand,
teach a sport with passion,
show children and young adults how to win with humility
and lose with dignity,
who remember to draw upon a graceful calmness
in those very frustrating and disappointing moments,
and who always remember that their athletes are just kids.

Teachers

A passionate teacher makes a difference.
Learning is effortless as this teacher reaches in
and sparks an awakening for reading, or science, or language.
Almost everyone can remember such a person in his or her life.

This would be a great time to pray for one of your teachers
who found the learner within you
or for a teacher who has done the same for a child you love.

Handmade

In a time with incredible technology,
there are people who work in professions
that haven't changed over time.
The violinmaker who handles wood with care
and ages the instrument for perfect sound,
the person who paints icons in the tradition of the masters,
the woodworker who uses tools like his great-grandfather,
the glassblower who repeats a process in his work
that men practiced centuries ago.
These people do not rush their work.
They feel an attachment to traditions of the past
and the beauty it brings to their craft.

Today, think about the handmade items
that cannot be improved upon by machines,
and thank a master craftsperson for keeping the traditions alive.

The Written and Spoken Word

Never has there been a point in history
where access to information and events
has been more instantaneous or plentiful.
We look to reporters, journalists, and political writers
for stories, details, and analyses of situations.
We expect complete reports of well-researched facts,
without personal bias or manipulation,
and summations drawn from critical appraisals.
Those who choose to weave personal agendas
and prejudices into their work,
who fabricate details for effect,
or ignore information that contradicts their point of view
have lost integrity in their craft.

For the reporters of information,
say a prayer for a clear view of their roles
as messengers and not interpreters
of the who, what, where, and how of the world around us.

The Rescuers

Today, say a prayer for those people
who rescue and care for neglected animals.
Whether it is their job,
or something they volunteer for,
they are performing a kind and wonderful service.

Manning the Polls

Whether it is a school board election each spring
or the presidential election every four years,
the same workers sit at the desks,
care for the books, and tend to the voting booths.
Recognizing that they are integral parts of the democratic process,
that we sometimes take for granted,
say a prayer of thanks for those who help make it work.

Patron of the Arts

Sometimes we see images of beautiful women in luxurious gowns,
handsome men in tuxedoes, massive floral arrangements,
and expensive champagne served on silver trays by uniformed butlers.
Sometimes, we question,
"How can this be when there are so many who are struggling
to make ends meet?"
It doesn't seem right. It doesn't seem fair.
What often doesn't get reported in the press is that
the people at those galas write checks for significant donations.
These contributions help museums purchase new acquisitions,
or continue programs which are free to the public or school children,
or they help pay salaries and expenses at non-profit organizations,
or buy dozens of cots for a shelter,
or medicine at a neighborhood clinic.
Very often these people make the difference
between shutting and keeping the doors open.

Instead of seeing only the glitz and glamour of the fund-raising event,
say a prayer of thanks
for the benefactor whose donations to a worthy cause make a difference.

Bye, Bye, Blackbird

It may not be the blackbird's time
but preservation groups report
that animals such as the cheetah, the angel shark,
the golden arrow poison frog,
manatees,
the northern right whales,
the Sumatran rhino, and the addax
are among those who are in danger of becoming extinct.
Changes in the planet cause changes in habitats,
which often affect the breeding and food supply of animals.
Other times, animal populations decline because of over-hunting.

For those individuals who monitor animal birth and survival rates
and who wave the red flag when numbers fall dramatically over time,
thank you for bringing the issues to our attention
and making us aware that extinction is not an option.

Chapter 5

For Perseverance

"May the Lord direct your hearts
into God's love and Christ's perseverance."
(2 Thessalonians 3:5)

Step by Step

There are fathers and then, there are stepfathers.
Sometimes a child only has the stepfather in his life,
sometimes he has both,
and sometimes there are problems.
Maybe there is tension between the child and stepfather,
maybe there is resentment,
maybe there is complete indifference,
but maybe, if all are lucky and have worked hard at the relationship,
there is none of the above.

For the stepfather who is trying to be a good parent,
and forge bonds with children who are not his own,
say a prayer of support and strength to persevere through difficult times.

Pink Slips

Massive unemployment is a national problem
but within the walls of a home,
just one person being unemployed can be a catastrophe.
Politicians debate strategies for solutions,
while the jobless debate what bills they can pay,
and where to cut costs.
Restructuring personal finances, rewriting resumes,
researching job postings, renewing contacts and networks,
all the while trying to maintain a sense of calm and optimism,
requires an inner strength to rise to the surface.

For one person without a job,
whether he or she is the primary breadwinner for a family,
the second very-much-needed income,
a single person,
a retiree supplementing a pension,
or a recent graduate who entered the job market
when the economy took a dive,
say a prayer.
Pray that this person remains confident and focused
during a very difficult time.

Single File

It was not her choice to be divorced, but she is.
It was not her idea to have the affair
that ended her marriage, it was her husband's.
Ex-husband.
She is not used to the idea of being divorced
and hesitates before checking it off in the "marital status" box.
It feels like it should read "betrayed and discarded,"
but that is not an option.
The path for her life shifted to another track;
one she never imagined would be hers.

Keep her in your prayers today, or someone just like her.
Maybe it is a "betrayed and discarded" husband.

False Witness

It takes courage for someone to live his life
when false accusations are made against him.
We are very used to hearing and reading about scandals,
white-collar crime, tax evasion,
date rape, and sexual misconduct
in connection with "pillars of the community."
Nothing seems to shock or surprise us.
But, what about when these accusations are entirely false?
The accused knows the truth,
but no matter how many times he states his innocence,
it is like screaming in a dream.
It is so difficult to get through each day
when you feel you are judged without evidence and guilty without proof.

Today, say a prayer for the innocent person
in the middle of accusations and finger pointing.
Pray that he finds a sense of calmness and peace
in the storm that surrounds him,
that he is granted grace for this day,
and the courage to hold his head up and focus his vision on the truth.

Overwhelmed

Sometimes, it's just too much.
All of it.
The job or lack of a job,
the marriage or lack of a marriage,
the bills, calls from creditors,
a feeling of hopelessness and helplessness.
There seems to be no blue in the sliver of sky
visible from the bottom of a very deep hole.
Suicide often seems the only way out
and today someone is considering this option, very seriously.

Today, pray for this person.
Pray he finds help with the burdens he carries,
that the darkness in his soul is erased.
Pray, he believes and trusts in hope again.

Parched

We hear about dry spells, low reservoirs, a shortage of rainfall,
but open a tap and water flows.
We brush our teeth,
wash our hair,
bathe in a deep tub,
take long hot showers,
do the laundry and the dishes
all with clean and abundant water.
There are places in Africa where severe drought
has been a way of life for decades.

Today, pray for someone living through another year without water.
Pray that rain eases the situation.

Claire Coleman

Missing in Action

Children under the age of eighteen
account for more than three-quarters of the tens of thousands
of people missing each year.
Are some of these runaways? Sure.
Are some of them taken by a parent? Sure.
But what about the others—
taken by strangers, rapists, sexual abusers,
serial killers.
The families must endure the terror and torment
of thoughts going through their heads
as they wait and pray for the safe return of their children.

Say a prayer today for one family
waiting for the missing piece of their lives to come home
and for those people who search for missing children.

The Worst Boss

If she could quit her job she would,
but the job market is tough right now,
so she stays at a place that she dreads each workday morning.
It's not the work,
it's the guy in the corner office
who makes life so miserable from nine to five.
Or eight to seven.
or seven to nine,
or whatever time he decides the workday begins and ends.
This boss verbally humiliates some, ridicules others,
and screams at everyone.

For the woman (or man) in a job with an abusive boss,
say a prayer to help her or him endure the situation
until she or he can get out.

The Child of an Alcoholic

A child with an alcoholic parent gets cheated in childhood.
Maybe he is hit once in a while,
maybe he is verbally abused,
or he has to watch as the other parent is beaten or terrorized.
Home is not a safe haven.
It is a wicked roller coaster ride
that can make violent twists and turns at any time,
without warning.
A child with an alcoholic parent often doesn't know
who or what to trust.
Sometimes the parent cares for him,
sometimes he cares for the passed out parent.
This kid grows up too soon and carries shame.

Your prayer of love and support for this child
may help him (or her) get through another day.

One for the Road

The spouses of alcoholics often feel like walking out on the situation,
especially a situation of repeated lapses by the drinking partner.
They try to be supportive, patient, loving, and caring
but the drinking creates such chaos in their lives.
Sometimes they want to get in the car
and drive until the gas tank is empty,
refill it and drive some more.
Some days they can't remember
when life wasn't littered with empty vodka bottles.

Say a prayer today for the person struggling not with the drink,
but with the drinker and the state of the life between them.
Say a prayer for perseverance
and the ability to find renewal and rest for soul and spirit
as he or she moves through another day.

Looking for Love

Even with on-line dating and matchmaking services,
some people, who want to be in a relationship,
are still alone.
They have tried to meet "someone"
through friends, through friends of friends,
at the singles' bars and clubs,
a summer singles' beach house,
blind dates, computer match-ups,
speed dating, faith-based singles' groups,
and once, in desperation, a personal ad.
But they are still without the relationship they crave.

Today say a prayer for the lonely hearted
who are looking hard for love.
Maybe one day soon, love will find them.

The Newly Diagnosed

Her mammogram shows a tumor
and her doctor is talking about surgery.
And chemotherapy.
And radiation.
All these words, these procedures, these treatments are a blur,
they swirl in the room where she sits with the doctor and the diagnosis.

Say a prayer for her today,
pray that the Lord reveals to her a courage deep within
and that she grasps it with both hands.

From This Day Forward

Snapshots of recent political scandals
include the dutiful wife, standing stone-faced,
slightly to the side of her husband.
As the "official statement" is read,
she sees only two options:
she can stare at him, but she fears her face would betray her thoughts
or
she can stare blankly into the tsunami-size wall of reporters,
technicians, camera people, camera flashes,
sound equipment, video recorders, and cell phone recorders
and try very hard to mentally disengage from the actual event.
A very personal, private matter between this couple
has become breaking news,
headline news, the evening news, and the news at eleven.
And then it starts again with the morning news.
Her mortification is palpable.
Whether it is a high profile or local issue that incriminates her spouse,
say a prayer for the woman who is innocent in the situation
and must stand by the man until judgment is passed.
This woman needs grace, support, and comfort
to bear up during this time in her life.

Waterworks

This family needs prayers and lots of them.
Floodwaters from a swollen river rose quickly
and rushed into their home.
When the water receded,
the interior of the house was barely recognizable.
Tables, chairs, and appliances stand piled against each other,
coated with red mud.
Now, black mold corrupts the rooms,
rugs, books, photo albums, pillows, furniture,
and grows behind the walls.
Cleaning up is physically and emotionally draining.
Day after day, working in filth
and trying to see some sort of light at the end of the tunnel
can erode the spirit of the most optimistic.
This family needs courage and hope today
and for many days to come.

"A" for Effort

Getting into college is a challenge.
Staying in can be an even bigger challenge for some.
For many, it is the first time they are away from home.
The first time there is no one looking over their shoulders
asking about homework deadlines,
making sure they don't oversleep, setting a curfew.
Maybe it's the first time they are exposed to so much drinking,
to drugs, to sex, to time and space of self-imposed boundaries.
They can play video games all day and night,
instead of going to classes, keeping up with their reading,
handing in assignments, finding study groups,
researching papers.
Temptations are there; choices must be made.

For new college students, a prayer for wisdom
in the choices they make
so that they remember the fundamental reason
they are on the college campus is to receive an education.

Make It Right

There are people who speak up
when they see an issue that needs to be addressed.
It might be seriously overcrowded classrooms
or mismanaged funds in a school district,
broken equipment at a factory, chemicals released into a water source,
health inspectors who take payoffs to ignore violations,
corruption within a police department,
false information which deliberately misleads shareholders,
or dozens of other situations where cheating,
lying, and stealing are permitted.
These people call attention to the problem and often work to correct it.
In some cases, showing up at a public hearing
and reading a statement
is enough to bring light to the issue.
Other times, they address government agencies
and hope someone there listens and acts.
As a last resort, some take their findings to the media.
Doing the right thing is the right thing to do,
but it often takes a whistle-blower to alert the public
to some very wrong things.
For the individual who stands up and speaks up
when a serious injustice takes place,
say a prayer of thanks and a strong prayer of support,
for often the battle to make others see and hear your message
is a long and lonely one.

Forgive and Forget

Today, say a prayer for the person trying to forgive
a spouse for having an affair.
It was discovered,
it ended,
there was counseling,
and on the surface, things are back to normal.
Some days, the betrayed partner only
goes through the motions
of being "one big happy family."
Those are the days when the hurt and humiliation,
thought to be exorcised, return as nagging distractions.

This business of forgiveness is not easy,
help this person with your prayer.

Land Mines

In some countries there are fields
where farmers could grow food
or where a school or a hospital could be built
but instead, barricades and warning signs fence it off.
The field is riddled with unexploded land mines.
There are people who continue to remind governments of this problem
and they work to have the fields cleared.
They work to bring attention to the issue.
They photograph the dead and maimed
to highlight the casualties of the hidden mines.
Because so many of the victims of land mines are children,
these people work tirelessly and with a sense of extreme urgency.

For those who see the horrific effects of land mines
and work to make a difference,
say a prayer of spiritual support and thanks.

Just Keep Saying No

The only way this mother can live in the same house
with her children is to stay off drugs.
The court tells her this, her family tells her this,
and she tells it to herself every morning and every night.
But the things that drove her to drugs in the first place,
find a way to come back and haunt her.
Sometimes at night, when loneliness echoes in her thoughts,
or at work when other women talk about their kids;
it seems too much to handle.
But she forces herself to remember the hell of withdrawal
and the sweetness of a child's good night kiss.

Today, say a prayer for this woman
as she struggles in her efforts
to stay clean one more day
and holds on to the image
of becoming a family under one roof again.

Accidents Happen

Accidents inevitably happen;
from the baseball that goes through a window
to bumpers that collide in a parking lot.
Big accidents happen, too.
Accidents that cause serious injuries or death.
For those responsible for such an accident,
life can never be the same.
There is guilt, shame, depression, anxiety
and maybe a withdrawal from social situations.
The thought that other people know about the accident they caused
and are talking about it behind their back
is more than they can face.
It doesn't matter if they were exonerated from blame,
they will blame themselves forever.
It doesn't matter if they have been forgiven,
they will never forgive themselves.
For the people who hold themselves responsible
for another's injuries,
say a prayer that they find strength, comfort,
and a way to move forward in their lives.

Chapter 6

Prayers and Intercessions

"I exhort therefore, that first of all,
supplications, prayers, intercessions,
and giving of thanks be made for all men."
(1 Timothy 2:1–4)

Hail to the Chief

The president of the United States deserves your prayer today.
Whether he is the person you wanted in the office or not,
he is still the president
and this is your country.

Say a simple prayer for the president—
for guidance, strength, and wisdom.

Think of a Country

Think of a country in the world.
Be specific (England) or vague (a small country in Central America).
Then say a prayer for the head of state in that country.
The world needs leaders who are wise, ethical, and moral.
The world needs leaders who are willing to serve the people.

Leaders who are trying to do this need our prayers.

The Undocumented

On a street corner in a city,
one man joins others waiting for a van or a pickup truck.
A nod from the driver means there is work today.
It could be in a field, on a landscape project,
for stonework, or for construction;
it doesn't matter, there is a job today and it is his.
He is most likely an immigrant without papers
and without malice toward the country
that helps keep his family fed.
There is always the fear that tomorrow there will be no work
or that his undocumented status will be discovered.
To some people, he is one part of the huge problem of illegal workers
and in their minds, deportation offers the only solution.
In his mind, he is working hard and long to feed his family
and give them a better life than in his old country.
He is the nameless center of a national issue.

Maybe, there is a solution—let us pray.

The Holocaust Survivor

Their numbers are dwindling
but the memories of camps, deprivation,
gas chambers, random executions,
the deaths of relatives and friends never fade.
Sometimes it seems like the world doesn't want to be reminded.

Say a prayer for Holocaust survivors,
that their mantra of "Never Again" is embraced even after they are gone.

Your Honor

The integrity of judges in our legal system
is critical to our democracy.
These men and women sit and listen
to evidence, testimonies, and arguments,
sustain and overrule objections,
instruct juries on points of law,
create environments
in which each defendant receives a fair trial,
where each plaintiff is heard,
where civil rights and liberties are protected,
and where the constitutionality of laws is debated.

For one judge—
whether he or she sits in traffic court or the Supreme Court,
say a prayer he or she always honors his or her sworn oath to the law.

Juries

Every working day in courtrooms across America,
men and women sit and listen to the charges, the evidence,
the testimonies, the prosecution and the defense,
and must determine
the guilt or innocence of an accused.
It is a right to be tried by a jury and a right to be part of one.

Today, say a prayer for the juries in the courtrooms across the country.
Say a prayer that their deliberations are made in good conscience
and the verdicts they deliver are fair and just.

Claire Coleman

Retired

Whether they worked for the same company for thirty-five years
or they worked five jobs in thirty-five years,
at some point,
the last day of work comes and goes.
Now they are officially retired.
The problem is they don't know what to do.
They are looking to fill the time with something
besides walking the dog in the morning,
grocery shopping in the afternoon,
and eating dinner while watching the six o'clock news.

Today say a prayer for the person
who hasn't adjusted to life without a job
and can't seem to find his or her way.

Moving Day

Hundreds, if not thousands, of people will be moving
into senior care facilities today.
Perhaps it is an assisted living complex
where the individual has
his own living quarters,
and his privacy is almost the same as when he lived at home.
Maybe it is a community-type environment
with private sleeping quarters but communal meals and activities.
For others, they will be moving into a full care nursing facility
where they will share a bedroom with a stranger,
and the only privacy is afforded by
a cotton curtain drawn at the discretion of the caregiver.
Everything is communal, privacy minimal.

For the senior who is moving into any one of these care facilities
knowing that this will be his last home, say a prayer.
Offer your thoughts and spiritual support that this person
is treated with respect and dignity in his new home,
and that he receives good care
and finds friendship among the other residents and staff.

Victims of the Prosecution

Their job is to prosecute criminals.
To do it well, they study the law
but they also study police reports
and crime scenes of murders,
rapes, beatings, child abuse.
They interact with depraved, cruel, sadistic, and violent human beings.

Sometimes it must be hard to remember
that life is not all victims and perpetrators.
Say a prayer today for someone who sees so much brutality.

A Lesson to Learn

A prayer for the coach who yells, screams, curses, and humiliates players.
A prayer that either he recognizes
how damaging his behavior is to young people and changes it,
gets help to change it,
or leaves the job.

Say a prayer for this coach
so he realizes the impact of a good coach on players
and the difference he can make in young lives.

World Traveler

Remember those old traveling salesmen jokes?
The untold story is that there is nothing funny about the lifestyle.
It has a very lonely side to it.
Every day, tens of thousands of business people
are on the road, or in the skies,
shuttling between home and their "territory."
Very often, they are doing it alone.

Say a short prayer today for the lonely traveler—
may his day be broken up by a cheerful soul in the next seat,
a friendly face at the check-in counter,
a great phone call from home,
and one of the best cups of coffee ever, in a most unexpected place.

The Traveler

Millions of people travel every day.
Some commute to work,
some are on business trips,
and some are getting away from work on a much-needed vacation.

Just say a quick prayer today
for someone on the road, on the rails, on the water, or in the air.
May he or she arrive safely at his or her destination.

Graduates

The months of May and June are filled
with college and high school graduation ceremonies
from one end of this country to the other.
Caps and gowns,
honors and awards,
honored guests, speakers and valedictorians,
caps in the air,
pictures and pictures and more pictures of these great moments.

For all the graduates this year in all the towns and cities,
offer a prayer for just one person.
As he or she enters a new phase of life
may the seeds of his or her dreams take root and begin to grow.

Poor Little Rich Girl

Her birthday parties cost more than some weddings,
her clothes budget more than what some people make in a year.
She has grown up with nannies, housekeepers, and cooks.
She never had to share a bedroom, make her own bed,
clean a bathroom, wash dishes, or do her laundry.
She knows a salad fork from a dinner fork
but not how to polish the sterling silver flatware
she will inherit.
She has trust funds, investment accounts,
and a checking account
funded with money someone else earned.
She wants to get a job like some of her friends,
but can't think of what to write on a resume.
She had summer vacations instead of summer jobs,
charity cotillions instead of charity work,
and knows fashion history instead of world history.

For the young woman who has lived a very "comfortable" life
but struggles with how to make a life of her own,
say a prayer for the ability to honestly look at herself
and draw upon what she needs to do to become her own person.

Chapter 7

Give Each Other Strength

"Encourage each other and give each other strength."
(1 Thessalonians 5:11)

A New Limb

Maybe it was a car accident, a mechanical malfunction at work,
or a consequence of the war,
but today someone is being fitted for an artificial limb.
Gone are the bones, the digits, the strength,
the flexibility, her own flesh.
All replaced with titanium and hinges.
Thankfully, technology offers a new limb with great dexterity
but it's still a man-made device.

Please say a prayer today for the person trying on a new limb.

First Day of School

There is someone who regrets dropping out of school.
He now realizes it was a mistake,
and that he will never get a better job without more education.
He knows he will need more skills,
more of the basics—reading, writing, and math
or he will remain locked into a series of dead-end jobs.
Going back to school is admitting a mistake,
and that is embarrassing.
This person needs strength in his heart to act.

Today, say a prayer for the person who struggles with the decision
to return to school and complete his education.
It is the right thing to do.
He needs encouragement to take the first step.
Be his prayerful support.

Lost and Found

Tens of thousands known as the Lost Boys of Sudan ran for their lives.
They escaped death in their villages
but knew their families were tortured and killed.
They moved from place to place,
sometimes only steps ahead of murderous gangs.
Even refugee camps weren't entirely safe havens,
and often the boys were forced to leave when threats resurfaced.
Thousands of these boys were brought to the US by relief agencies
where they were welcomed into families.

Today say a prayer for one of the Lost Boys
as he adjusts to life in this country,
or one of the boys who remained behind in Sudan,
or for the people in the international agencies
who saw the desperation of these boys
and planned and organized their emigration to America,
or one of the families who brought them into their fold.

Losing a Child

Ask any parent for their worst nightmare
and they will say the same thing:
losing a child.
Millions of parents live this nightmare.
Whether a stillbirth, an accident, illness,
or disease cut short the life of their child,
the scar lies atop their heart and within their soul.
If you do not know anyone this has happened to,
consider yourself lucky,
because chances are that someone you pass on the street,
speak to on the phone,
exercise with at the gym,
is among those heartbroken parents.

Every day they need prayers for healing
and the strength to get through the day.

Claire Coleman

One Day at a Time

Through Alcoholics Anonymous thousands of men and women
overcome their addiction to alcohol.
But it is a struggle each day to stay away from a drink.
They support one another, they believe in a higher power,
and they take one day at a time.

Say a prayer today for the recovering alcoholic,
who maintains a self-controlled life,
knowing that the out-of-control life is only one drink away.

A Single Dad with Sons

He is a single dad with boys to raise.
The easy part has been what he always saw himself doing as a dad—
throwing baseballs and footballs,
showing them how to mow a lawn,
wash a car, wash the dog, and take out the garbage.
The harder part is everything else.
Knowing when a sore throat might be strep,
remembering to send birthday treats to school for the youngest one,
getting them to use a napkin instead of the back of their hand,
getting them to church,
trying to see what video games they are playing,
and what type of websites they are visiting.
And soon there will be talks about girls, drinking, and drugs.
The list of worries for this single dad is very long.

Today say a prayer for him or someone just like him
who is trying his very best at a very tough job.

Growing Pains

Acne, voice changes, body changes, parents who don't understand,
chemistry lab, geometry, being too old for toys, too young for cars,
teachers who don't understand,
trying to make the team, weight issues, sex, drugs, rock and roll,
and trying to find out who you are.
These things are only part of why no one envies teenagers.
Their footing in the world seems to shift, sink, and falter
as they deal with family, academics, sports,
relationships with friends and with friends of the opposite sex,
disappointments, authority, independence,
loneliness, physical and emotional changes, anger management,
peer pressure, curiosity about drugs and sex,
body image and food issues, and questions about their faith.
Add to this, the burden of poverty,
divorced or abusive parents
that some young people also have to deal with,
and there is a realization that getting through the teen years
can be a Herculean struggle of mind, body, and spirit.
Keep in mind a teenager today,
a struggling one or one who seems to have all the answers.
They all are struggling—some are just more obvious than others.

Listen to This

Today someone is slowly but surely becoming permanently deaf.
Male or female, very young, middle-aged, or elderly.
This individual now faces a harsh fact.
It is frightening, sad, and overwhelming to deal with this news.
Technology can help a few people with some of the hearing loss
but not all of it.

For the person who has to listen to this news today,
say a prayer so that she is given strength to deal with this issue
and that in the near future research will bring about some hope for her.

Boy, Oh Boy!

Boys, boys, everywhere
and not a drop of pink.
Her sons have filled her home with
everything from trucks, trains, and tricycles
to hockey sticks, baseball mitts, football pads, and soccer cleats.
She thought there was supposed to be time
somewhere between her job,
and keeping food in the house,
driving them to their games,
washing clothes,
delegating chores,
and checking homework,
to teach them about manners,
listen to their concerns or anxieties,
ask them about girls and dating,
and bond with them like the parenting books describe.
For the single mother of boys
who wants unstructured time with each son
to discover the soul of the man he will become,
say a prayer for patience and wisdom.

Break Away

In a city somewhere, a young man wants to leave his gang.
He finally sees that this is not the path he should be taking.
He wants to stay in school.
He really wants to go to college.
He wants to move from the violence, the drugs, and the crime,
but it is very difficult.
The gang, once his brotherhood, now feels like a vice,
squeezing hope from his soul.
He feels threatened and worries about whether he can break free from it.

Say a prayer he makes it.

The Birth Day

She gave her baby up for adoption
because she was either too young or too poor,
lacked family support or the means to support a family,
needed to finish high school or start high school.
There are hundreds of reasons
why mothers surrender their babies to other people.
Once a year the birth mother faces the birth day
and she wonders where her baby is,
what he looks like, what were his first words,
his favorite toys and books,
if his parents love him enough,
and would she recognize him if she saw him somewhere.
The questions remain after the birth day is over.

For one birth mother today,
who has a piece of her heart
living somewhere, some other town, some other state,
say a prayer for comfort and peace with a difficult decision
she made years ago for very personal reasons.

Night Owl

People going to night school need prayers.
They work regular jobs and take classes at night
to complete either their high school or college degrees,
or maybe a master's, a doctorate, or law degree.
Their discretionary time has shrunken dramatically
while they stay on their mission to complete this part of their education.

Say a prayer for the strength to finish.

Claire Coleman

When a Pet Dies

For many people, their pets are like family members,
so when the pet has to be put down
the grief and loss cut deep into their hearts.
Letting go of that faithful companion is truly heart rendering
but how silly it seems to say, "I'm so sad because my dog died."
But the grief is very real.

Say a prayer today so that someone mourning the loss of a pet
will find comfort in the days ahead.

A Decision to Change

Today, pray for just one very heavy person
who believes he cannot change,
and that all the talk and chatter
about diet and exercise will not work for him.
He has given up trying to change.
Today, pray that some ember of hope glows strong enough
to spark motivation within him.
Becoming healthy after years of self-neglect
will take a new decision,
a steadfast commitment,
patience, time, and self-love.

It is a long road for this person
so consider repeating this prayer
each day for months;
you are praying for someone who really needs it.

For Better or Worse

In the marriage vows, each partner promises
to stay committed to each other "for better or for worse."
What happens when "the worse" happens?
A catastrophic accident or illness and suddenly the marriage changes
from two partners to an invalid and a caretaker.
One spouse is called upon to make good on that vow.

Today, say a prayer for this spouse as he or she tries
with every ounce of strength, compassion, and love
to uphold his or her end of the deal.

Disturbing the Peace

Someone broke into a home,
emptied drawers,
threw aside what was on the desk,
on the dresser and in the closets,
then took what he wanted.
He took some money or some jewelry
or all the money and all the jewelry.
He left behind a sense of violation, anger, and loss,
a sense of vulnerability in the homeowner,
that the person never felt before.

Say a prayer today for someone who has been burglarized
and must live with the pain of it.

Claire Coleman

The Parents of a Bipolar Child

The bipolar diagnosis was stunning,
but made perfect sense considering the facts.
The parents were assured by the professionals
that there was nothing they did
to cause the situation.
But, they can't help but wonder
what caused a beautiful cherub-faced baby
to take a neurological turn in the road.
The doctors, the psychiatrists, the reports,
the medications, the hospitalizations,
and the label placed on the child as a verbal tattoo
overwhelm them on even the best of days.

For the parents of a bipolar child
say a prayer of support
and also, that as they find all the necessary help for their child,
they find the very necessary help and guidance for themselves.

Losing Sight

No doctor needs to tell him what he knows in his heart.
It is clear that his sight is failing
and it will be completely gone in two years.
He is frightened and saddened by the losses to come—
the sight of a blue sky,
the crimson and gold of autumn foliage,
the smile of a child,
the interaction with art,
the sight of his wife.
He worries about how blindness will affect his plans
to remain in his house,
drive his car,
manage his finances,
and have a social life.
He fears becoming dependent on others
and a burden to his family
more than he fears his blindness.
Today, say a prayer for this man.
May he find ways to cope with what is changing his life.
May grace allow him to accept help from others
without fear of dependency.

Claire Coleman

Siblings

Parents of men and women on active military duty
have fears and emotions with which all parents can identify.
But the bonds between siblings are also special.
For these siblings, watching your big brother, your twin,
your kid sister go off to war is painful.
Whether the service person is one of ten children or two,
there are the siblings who wait and pray for his or her safe return.

Say a prayer today for the siblings who count down the days
until they get to give their buddy,
their first roommate,
their friend
a great, big hug.

Bachelor Father

A single dad with a family of daughters needs a prayer today.
He is trying his best but sometimes he is overwhelmed
by all that has to be done,
the advice he receives from family and friends,
and the doubts about his parenting skills that creep into his mind.
He works hard to do his best by his girls.

Pray for this man
so he may parent his daughters
with wisdom, understanding, and confidence.

Take a Chance on a Cure

Disaster relief, war widows, war orphans, the poor in this country,
or in third world countries, animal rights, cancer research,
inner-city youth programs, clean air and water,
and the list goes on and on.
We hear persuasive pitches for money every day.
But we also hear and see the families of children
with cancer, cystic fibrosis, juvenile diabetes, muscular dystrophy,
cerebral palsy, autism, spina bifida and rare neurological conditions
as they invite us to join and support their cause.
They write letters, organize bake sales, spaghetti dinners.
They ask for donations outside supermarkets on blistering hot days,
and on days of torrential downpours.
They sell raffle tickets and 50/50 tickets, sign up sponsors for walk-a-thons,
read-a-thons, swim-a-thons, bike-a-thons, marathons, and 5K races.
And all the while, time may be running out for their child and a cure.
They would sell their soul for a cure.
In the meantime, they try to convince friends, neighbors, and strangers
that of all the good causes out there,
this one really needs your help.
For the fundraising parents who are working against time,
say a prayer for the good they are doing,
then drop some money in the bucket and buy a chance.

To Go or Not to Go

He is the first one in his family with the grades,
the opportunity,
and the encouragement of teachers
to go to college.
But his parents want him to stay,
get any job,
and help the family with the bills.
They fear that if he leaves for school
he will never return.
They fear he will be ashamed of them and their lack of education.
He loves his family but their disapproval is hurtful and confusing.
This boy needs courage to follow his heart
and block out selfish attempts to make him stay.

Say a prayer for the courage to follow a dream and a journey,
even if it means doing it alone.

Baby Tears

Today say a prayer for the couple who want to have a baby.
Their intimate moments, once private and personal,
have become organized, orchestrated, documented,
and shared with a team of health care professionals.
Privacy left months ago.
Each month the anticipation builds and falls,
only to build again the next month.
This maddening cycle creates tension
between two people who just want the same thing:
a baby.

Pray that soon this husband and wife become father and mother.

Nine to Five, Five to Nine

For the person working two jobs,
a day seems longer than twenty-four hours.
Between stepping out of bed before dawn
and climbing back in at midnight,
there is an endless stretch of hours
devoted to getting those two paychecks.
Some people do this to reduce debt,
buy a house,
save for the kids' education,
create a retirement fund,
finance a business,
or meet the costs of everyday life.
Few would choose this life if they didn't have to.
A prayer today for the worker who handles two jobs
and handles the rest of life in between.

Face Forward

Whether she was born with a facial deformity
or had an accident that caused it,
something has made her face different,
odd, unusual, distorted, scarred, or almost hideous.
It can be so difficult to be in public;
small children stare, point, or call out the obvious
while some adults refuse to make eye contact.
Rare is the person who does make eye contact
and doesn't stare or shun interaction.

For the person who lives with a disfigurement
and faces the reactions of others
every day of her life,
say a prayer for self-acceptance
and courage as she goes about her life.

Number Cruncher

Today, a man faces an opportunity
to change of few numbers in the books of his company.
A shifting of facts, a little "creative accounting"
and he can add some extra money to his own account.
It will just be this one time, he thinks,
just to get through this streak of bad luck.
He is behind in all his payments
and seriously in debt because of his gambling obsession.
He stares at the numbers,
knowing exactly how to pull this off without anyone suspecting a thing.

Pray for him today.
Pray that his sense of right and wrong will prevail,
that he will remember that honesty stirs in his soul.
Pray he gets help for his problem.

The Multi-tasker

Single mothers do it all,
or at least they go down trying to do it all.
Offer a prayer of support for the woman who has to be mom and dad,
wage earner and bill payer,
laundress,
grocery shopper,
homework expert,
school volunteer,
team parent,
confidante, and child psychologist.
Hopefully, the best she can do today will be good enough
for the ones she is doing it for and for herself.

Offer a prayer of support for this one-woman show.

Chapter 8

For Unfailing Faith

"... But I have prayed for you
that your faith should not fail ..."
(Luke 22:31–32)

One of a Kind

It is a school day and teachers are entering classrooms.
Some have clean blackboards,
a crisp American flag hanging in the corner,
and a bulletin board layered with seasonal decorations.
Then there are other classrooms that have no chalk,
are over-crowded, poorly furnished,
and are vandalized regularly.
But still, the teachers teach,
even as the winter air streams through a broken pane,
even as budget cuts further reduce the opportunities for field trips,
hands-on material, movies, and the small "extras"
that help bring lessons to life.

For a teacher in an inner city or a poor rural area,
say a prayer of thanks for his or her commitment
to teaching against great odds.

Grand Opening

By the time he secured the money, the building,
the equipment, the suppliers,
a company logo, and his business cards for his own business,
the economy had taken a downturn and a bad one.
Now saddled with levels of debt that keep him awake at night,
he must continue this business
because there is no turning back and failure is a devastating option.
He is pulling all his strength, his creativity,
and his will from deep within himself to make the business work.

For the business owner struggling to breathe life into his livelihood
while markets are bad, money tight, and customers hard to come by,
say a prayer for faith in himself,
and a prayer that he survives the tough times and realizes his dream.

The Tough Fight

Some medical professionals have chosen to specialize in oncology
and take on the task of conquering and curing cancer.
Then there are those within that group who
specialize in pediatric oncology.
Every day that a child is diagnosed with cancer
there is a doctor, a nurse, lab technician,
chemotherapy specialist, and researcher,
among dozens of other support personnel,
literally and figuratively standing by that child's side.

Say a prayer of deep gratitude for every one of those specialists
who dedicate themselves and their work
to helping children survive an interrupted childhood.

Guilty by Association

In a country where we presume innocence,
why are so many still guilty by association?
This priest, this rabbi, this minister never defiled a child,
could never consider such thoughts,
yet when he put his arm around a young boy recently
he got "the look" from someone in the congregation.
He did nothing wrong,
he is not among the perverse abusers in the religious vocations,
but he feels suspicion directed at him.

Say a prayer for this man today
so that he might continue his life of service
without shadows cast upon his intentions and actions.

The Calling

Despite bad press and negative public opinion,
there are still men and women
who choose to commit to a life in a religious ministry.
A deep faith, coupled with an instinct that inspires action,
brought them to this decision.

Thank God for the person willing to serve Him and others.

Keeping the Faith

The minister's spouse shares her mate with a congregation.
Sometimes she handles a large dose of single-parenthood,
while the minister lectures on good parenting skills.
Even the most involved spouse
still has many hours alone
while the minister's days and nights are filled with meetings,
services, budget discussions, and more meetings.
Sometimes there is precious little time together.
The minister's spouse keeps the faith,
but there are moments when it is not so easy.

Say a prayer today for the supportive spouse
who needs some support to ward off feelings
of playing second fiddle to the minister's congregation.

Claire Coleman

Inter-faith Marriages

They believe what they have in common trumps their differences.
They believe love brought them together and will keep them together.
They believe they must spend the rest of their lives with each other.
They believe in different Gods
and their families believe their marriage will eventually fail.
Say a prayer today for those entering an inter-faith marriage,
that the grace they each receive allows them to create a life
of mutual respect and understanding.
Perhaps two faiths living peacefully under one roof
will be an example
to others of what is possible
when there is love of God and love of neighbor.

One Step at a Time

Years ago, children born with spina bifida
remained in wheelchairs their entire lives.
Today some walk, with braces, but they are walking nonetheless.

For the baby born today with spina bifida
and the family who receives this crushing news,
say a prayer of comfort and hope
that walking with braces is the beginning of many breakthroughs
for children with this condition.

The Waiting Game

For those who wait for an organ transplant,
it is a race against time.
When given months to live,
the minutes move in double-quick time.
It is a contest where the stakes are very high.

Today, say a prayer that the waiting game is over
for someone as news of a perfect donor is located.

Good Grief

There are people who specialize in grief,
but in a good way.
They are grief counselors and they help others
handle the unimaginable,
the inevitable,
the overwhelming
losses in their lives.
Some people shut out grief
while others never move from its grasp.
For these people and others, the grief counselor is a guide.

Say a prayer of thanks for grief counselors
who assist us through a devastating, painful experience
and show us how to live again.

Children Are Waiting

There are still children waiting to be adopted.
Forget the old images of small beds in neat rows with sad-eyed toddlers.
The children waiting in this country to be adopted are all ages:
three, eight, twelve, fifteen,
some with physical disabilities, some with emotional issues,
all needing love and stability.

Today, pray for the child who waits and waits.
Pray that for one child the waiting is over.

Chapter 9

Imprisoned

"Remember those who are in prison,
as though you were in prison with them."
(Hebrews 13:3)

The Chair

Think about people confined to wheelchairs.
Regardless of what put them there,
a stroke, an accident, a disease,
they are relegated to the chair.
For thousands of people, there is no relief from it.
No getting up and walking away,
no climbing up the stairs,
no standing in a hot shower,
no driving a car without special accommodations
Even the curb at the sidewalk's edge is a challenge.
There is no end in sight.

Today, please say a prayer for people in wheelchairs
who have no option to leave it.
They miss the ground beneath their feet,
the feel of sand, spring grass, and walking through puddles.
Pray that they are given the grace to live
without resentment and bitterness
at the rest of the walking world.

A Lifer

Today, say a prayer for a murderer,
someone who took the life of someone else,
either accidentally or with premeditation.
He sits in a jail cell
and will stay there for the next twenty years or, perhaps,
the rest of his life.
What can the prayer be for this man?
Perhaps, that he asks for forgiveness from God,
who will always bestow forgiveness.
Perhaps, then pray that he will forgive himself
and despair will never settle in his heart.
Pray that while in prison he becomes a better person than he was before.
Perhaps he will improve the lives of those with whom he is imprisoned,
as a way of compensating for removing a life from this world.

Claire Coleman

A Shut-In

Every town has shut-ins,
those individuals who, for health reasons, are confined to their homes.
It is difficult to be involuntarily locked out from a social life
and depend on others for your basic needs,
feeling like a marginal part of society and a burden to others.
But for some there is no choice.
How wonderful it would be even to go to the grocery store!
Seeing people other than those on TV,
talking with people rather than typing to them on computers,
and walking outside on the street or in a park
make a person feel a part of the day rather than apart from it.

Today, say a prayer for the shut-in
who longs to be someplace other than where she is.

Sold

Imagine being a fourteen-year-old girl in Asia
who is sold by her father
for a few hundred dollars.
The father needs money because the crops have failed
and he has too many children to feed.
A man tells the father his daughter will have a good job in a city factory.
The deal is made, but there is no factory job in reality.
Within forty-eight hours of leaving her parents and siblings,
this young girl is having unprotected sex with strange men.
This is her new life
and her family will probably never hear from her again.
There are thousands of young girls and young boys locked into this life,
with little chance of escape.
Most likely they will die of AIDS.

Can we truly imagine how desperate they feel,
and how bleak their future seems?
These young victims need a prayer today.
Let life turn a corner for them at some point.
Let them escape their captivity and have a future of their own.

The Anger Within

There are people who dwell in anger.
They find it impossible to forgive a parent, sibling,
spouse, child, or friend
for an incident, a word, a slight,
and they chose to stay within the realm of anger.
Forgiveness is hard to extend
especially when you feel justified as the victim,
as the hurt one.
However, being mired in anger corrodes the soul in time.

Think of the destruction of anger within someone,
maybe someone you know well,
and pray that he or she will find the way out of his or her torment
by accepting forgiveness as the solution
and valuing peace over indignation.

Tied to Home

It's called agoraphobia
and people who experience it fear situations outside their homes.
Many do not leave their homes for years.
They are trapped by irrational fears for their safety
and anxiety about the unknown.
The world is going by and they are watching it
from behind the bay window in the living room.
With some help, these people could step outside,
feel the sunshine, the rain, a soft breeze,
smell a freshly cut lawn or lilacs in the spring.
With some help they could see what lies beyond the bend.

Say a prayer today so that someone suffering with this
might get the help she needs
to begin living her life outside of her own four walls.

Good Days and Bad Days

Someone with multiple sclerosis defines his or her week
by the number of good days and bad days.
Good days, every once in awhile, have moments
when it is almost possible to forget,
just for a brief time, that this disease dominates your life.
Bad days, always, are filled with struggles
and the feeling that nothing is normal about your life.
MS symptoms strike the body with muscle weakness, spasms,
vision problems, and/or neuropathic pain.
Anxiety and depression come to the front
when symptoms increase in severity.
There is no escape from the erratic undertow of the disease.

Perhaps, one day, research will unlock the mystery of the disease
and find a cure.
In the meantime, pray for the person who suffers
through the disabilities of MS.

Child Labor

Instead of walking to school in the morning,
she walks into a factory.
The sun is not up, and it will set before she is allowed to leave.
Her job is at a sewing machine
where she works quickly, stitching seams together,
putting in a zipper, turning back the hem.
She works fast and finishes dozens of jackets each day.
If she were paid by the piece instead of per diem,
she would be happier
because she could bring more money to her mother.
But things could be worse;
she could be hunched over a cutting table
in the other part of the factory.
At least she has a chair.

Whether the little one who labors is a young girl or boy,
say a prayer that she or he has an opportunity
to leave the factory, go to school, and get a real job.

Claire Coleman

Never-Ending Pain

A pain in the neck.
Or lower back, or knees, or feet, or hands.
Millions of people live each day in chronic pain.
Medication helps at times, but not always.
They are in pain from the time they get up
to the time they get back into bed at night.
For many, the pain continues through the night
and then tomorrow dawns, and the pain is still there.

For someone who suffers with severe pain, in every step or every breath,
say a prayer that somehow his or her burden
will be lessened or lifted in time.

There Are No Words

Trauma to the brain either from an accident or a stroke
can often leave the individual aphasic.
Her ability to speak and/or comprehend language is impaired.
Sometimes she says the right words but in the wrong order,
or says the right words and wrong words in the same sentence.
Sometimes the sentences contain a mix of real words and gibberish.
Sometimes all the words are all gibberish,
barely intelligible sounds with no meaning.
Unfortunately, the speaker often has no clue that
what she has said cannot be understood.
Frustration rises on both sides of the "conversation."

Today, remember someone who has lost the gift of speech.

Chapter 10

The Suffering

"Remember those who are suffering,
as though you are suffering as they are."
(Hebrews 13:3)

Claire Coleman

Staying in the Shadows

There may be people in your office you rarely speak to,
people in your town you nod to but never say hello.
They are the background people,
seemingly content to be without a voice
and in the margins of our busy lives.
Maybe they are very shy, or elderly,
or not very handsome or pretty,
or the cat lady, or the guy with the limp.
Maybe they have acquiesced to the lesson
that they are not the sort of people
who are in the spotlight, the limelight,
or the front-runner, the leading lady.
Maybe their voice isn't so much silent as it is unwelcome or uninvited.

Today say a prayer for someone so shy and retiring
that she barely leaves a footprint on the earth.
Perhaps very soon, she is stopped by someone
who is willing to engage her and chat about something,
even if only to talk about sports or the weather,
and she will know someone out there is listening.

It's Not Personal

It's hard to say which is worse:
being fired as part of a ten percent cut in a major corporation
or being fired as part of the ten percent in a small company.
Sharing the pain with others offers only temporary comfort.
At the end of the day, there's still no job,
and the prospects of finding another are often so daunting.
Today, pray for one person who was fired
in a sweeping, impersonal lay-off.
Pray that as he goes through feelings
of sadness, anger, frustration,
self-recrimination, and heartbreak,
his spirit reminds him of his self-worth,
his strongest qualities and strengths,
and that being fired wasn't personal,
it was just business
during a very long and difficult recession.

The "Why" and the "What If . . ."

"Why did he do it?"
"Why didn't he talk to me?"
"Why didn't I see it coming?"
Why? Why? Why? Why?
Questions stream into the mind of a parent of a suicide victim
like incessant chatter.
There is endless self-blame, accusations, and disbelief.
There is also the ransacking of memories and events
for possible clues to the suicide state of mind.
The parents' souls are impaled by grief and anguish
leaving them with numb bodies
that somehow still manage to walk, talk, and go to work.

These mothers and fathers can't escape
the questions and the sorrows.
Today, please say a heartfelt prayer
for deep comfort, understanding, and peace
to heal the fractured souls and spirits of parents
who believe comfort, understanding, and peace
will never touch them again.

A Common Bond

He was your co-worker, your college friend, or maybe your first love
and news of his sudden death has reached you.
Shock, sadness, and hundreds of memories come into your heart.
You live too far to visit his widow.
You sent a note and a charitable donation.
He meant so much to you at one point in your life
that the loss continues to hang in your thoughts
for days and weeks.
You can only imagine the tremendous void in the family,
a widow and children you never met.

For the family and relatives of someone once very close to you,
say a prayer as they deal with their pain and grief.

A Shoulder to Cry On

It is only when someone close to her asks
about her mother, that she can honestly talk about
what it is like to see Alzheimer's dismantle the woman
who was wife, mother, aunt, grandmother, friend, co-worker.
Once in a while the daughter sees a tiny sign
that her mother recognizes her.
Once in a while, there is a flash of clarity in those lost eyes
or something in the way she reaches for her daughter's face
or squeezes her hand
that says, oh yes, you are mine.
But then it is gone.
The daughter shares this with only the closest of friends
because she cries when she speaks of it.
Thank goodness for friends.

For the daughter (or son) who knows that the parent-child bond
is thinning because of Alzheimer's,
say a prayer today of support and love.

Child's Play

A child's play was interrupted
when a bomb went off near the soccer field.
He was practicing with friends when the ground shook beneath his feet,
and clods of dirt and debris slammed sharply into his body.
It took him three agonizing minutes
to realize the blood on his arms and legs was not his own.
He was sitting on the field, hugging his knees,
and rocking back and forth when his father found him.
He is afraid to return to the field, even with his father beside him.
A war between nations, a war between tribes, a war between ideologies,
a war between angry mobs of men
creates casualties among the youngest survivors.

Say a prayer today for the young child touched by the sharpness of war.
Let it be a prayer for healing today
and for every day that memories haunt the innocent.

Scarred

Far from other wings in the hospital,
layered behind a series of restricted access doors
is the burn center.
Lying in one of the beds in the burn center
is someone with multiple, horrible, scarring burns.
The actual burning flesh was less painful than the months of recovery.
Enduring dressing changes, skin grafts, and physical therapy
defines the word excruciating.
There are psychological and emotional scars that must also heal.

Say a prayer today for a burn victim.

Bad Break

Today someone is dealing with a broken bone
and all the pain and frustrations it brings.
Whether it is a minor break, like a finger or a toe,
or considerable, like an ankle or wrist,
or major, like an arm, shoulder, hip, or leg,
it is difficult to get around,
get washed,
get dressed,
get meals prepared,
get food to a table,
get to work,
and even get to sleep.

For the person at the very beginning
of this broken bone experience,
say a prayer that he has patience with his limitations
and that he can ask for and accept help
where and when it is needed.

Claire Coleman

Rest for the Weary

For someone living with chronic fatigue syndrome
the days weigh heavy, and something as simple as making breakfast
is a mighty chore requiring effort and stamina.
It may take hours between thinking about making the food and eating it.
Then there is clean-up, another major task.
If breakfast is this complicated,
a commute to work and a job in an office is out of the question.
A single person with CFS may move back home
or hire help for the cooking, shopping, and cleaning.
For a married person, it may mean stretching one income
where there had been two.
For a married person with children,
it means the spouse does double duty
and the kids help as best they can.

For the person living with chronic fatigue syndrome,
say a prayer that she does not fall prey to depression,
and that more medical understanding about the causes and cures
helps those who have it now and
prevents others from ever having it.

Wrong Place, Wrong Time

He was just walking through the courtyard to his apartment
but it was the wrong place at the wrong time,
and he fell to a bullet meant for someone else.
He had trouble with no one,
avoided the gangs as much as possible,
and yet walked into the crosshairs of their violence.
His parents, his siblings, his friends cannot accept this tragedy
except, they know he is one of many
who died in the same way.

For the parents, siblings, cousins, and friends,
please pray that the greatest comfort the Lord can give
is gifted to them as they struggle with this loss.

As the Crow Flies

If given superman's x-ray vision
to look at your town or neighborhood
you might be able to identify the house
where cancer dominates.
This house might look like the others from the street
but it is where cancer and its life-robbing properties
hang in the air and dissolve joy.
Only one family member has cancer
but the whole family carries it upon their shoulders
and in the pits of their stomachs.
Sometimes they can talk about it but
other times they pretend it does not exist.
Often the reality of it arrives like a ghost in the night
and feeds anxious thoughts and quiet tears.

For those who live in the house with cancer,
say a prayer for personal peace, calmness, and health.

Breath of Fresh Air

For someone with a severe breathing disorder
taking a deep breath is a tall order.
Asthma, emphysema, pulmonary fibrosis,
lung cancer, pneumonia, and COPD,
are things that prevent a person from filling up his lungs.
Without those deep breaths, oxygen in the blood is lowered.
Sometimes there is such tightness in his chest
that it brings on anxiety or panic attacks.
Breathing is a gift we don't always think about
until all we can think about
is how hard it is to breathe.

For someone with serious health issues causing labored breathing,
say a prayer for relief, or at the very least, some comfort.

The Fat Kid

At some point, cute baby fat turns into just fat
and the child suffers.
His health suffers and his self-image suffers.
Other kids tease the fat kid.
It's been the way of the playground world for a long time.
Someone in control needs to take control.
Someone needs to take away the junk food,
the oversize portions of food,
and the mentality that is blind to the facts and fat before everyone's eyes.
Someone needs to help this child
before he develops irreversible health issues.

For one very overweight child today,
say a prayer that someone who loves him or her
will love enough to take control of the situation.

Survivor Guilt

They got out of the towers and the Pentagon with their lives.
But so many others on Tuesday, September 11, 2001 didn't.
Some who died were co-workers, business associates, competitors,
the guy who shined shoes, the lady with the coffee wagon.
Who knew survivor's guilt could feel so awful and for so long?

Today, say a prayer for someone who survived one horror
only to be cursed with another.

Claire Coleman

Pain in the Neck

Every day someone is living with fibromyalgia and there is no real rest.
In fact, often rest makes the pain worse, so sleep is fitful and disjointed.
There is muscle pain, sore points in the neck, shoulders, and back.
The aches and pains make it feel like a chronic case of the flu.
The large majority of the three to six million sufferers are women.
They have bad days with pain and some not as bad,
but they are never free of it.

Today say a prayer for this person in constant pain,
perhaps you can be the spiritual friend
to whom she can turn to for support and empathy.

The Decision

There is a decision to be made
and it is the most difficult anyone can imagine.
The spouse or parent or child is on life support
with no hope of life without it.
The decision to arrest the mechanical breathing
and let death takes this soul is agonizing,

This family needs a prayer today
to deal with the heartache of the situation before them.

Diabetics

Insulin does not cure diabetes.
How many people really know that?
It is a big disease without a cure.
Diabetics manage it with insulin but even that can be tricky.
Attention to diet is essential
because food can be the enemy.
Wounds and bad circulation can lead to amputations.
Kidney failure can occur.
Blindness is an ever-present threat.

Please say a prayer today for someone with diabetes,
who must monitor and adjust the blood sugar levels in his or her body
many times during the day, every day,
because his or her life depends on it.

Broken Heart

Parents of terminally ill children have divided hearts.
One half longs for more time with their child,
valuing each day as a gift
but, knowing that each day also draws them closer to an inevitable end.
The other half of the heart longs to see their child without pain,
and knows the only way this will happen is when the disease finally wins.
The two halves of this type of heart cannot beat without aching.

Parents of terminally ill children need all the prayers we can give them.

The Night Before

No one slept well last night.
It was the night before the first round of chemotherapy.
The hours dragged on and the anxieties multiplied.
No matter what the doctor said, what the nurse said,
what the pages of "what to expect" said,
it still felt like standing backstage at a horror show
and knowing you're about to be the main character in the drama.
But this is for real.
Cell-killing chemicals to be pumped into the veins,
then fatigue, nausea, and hair loss.

Today, say a prayer for the person standing on the brink of this journey.

Battered and Bruised

There is a man who beats his wife.
And he does it often.
He says it's her fault. It's always her fault.
Sometimes he doesn't touch her,
but he has mastered verbal abuse
to the point where she feels internally comatose.
This man needs to be removed from her life
before he becomes a wife killer.

Today, prayers are needed to help them both.
Pray that the Lord places the right people in their paths today,
whether family or police or social workers,
someone who will interrupt this horror.
Pray that he is healed of the demons that fuel his anger,
his need for domination and physical violence.
Pray that she is healed of all her wounds,
internally, externally, and psychologically.

Beaten Down

There is a wife who beats her husband.
And she does it often.
He cannot control or escape her rage
and feels like the wimp she tells him he is.
What shame and guilt he carries.
He feels there is no one to tell
without being exposed as a pathetic person.

So much help is needed here and so many prayers.
Pray for an intervention to separate this couple and healing for all.

HIV

Who can say which is the bigger shock,
the diagnosis of being HIV positive
or the vision of what lies ahead life?
Maybe only someone who has faced the issue knows the answer.
The examinations, the blood test, the pharmaceuticals (and the cost),
the yoke of this disease now squarely across his shoulders
and thrust into the center of his thinking.

Today someone is beginning to learn how to cope with this disease.
Say a prayer.

Claire Coleman

Forced to Submit

There are places in the world
where young girls are forced to submit
to genital mutilation,
a brutal, barbaric, and antiquated practice.
There are men and women
who insist that this custom must continue
despite the fatalities that often occur.
There are also men and women
who insist that this custom must cease
despite tradition and beliefs.
There are men and women
who secretly arrange for their daughters
to leave their villages or even their countries
rather than be brutalized.

For those who continue to educate the world
about female genital mutilation
and their efforts to arrest its practice, say a prayer of thankfulness.
For those traumatized by this custom, say a prayer for healing.

Twisted

Walking,
turning a door knob,
opening the refrigerator,
pouring coffee, cutting food on a plate,
writing with a pen, using a keyboard,
tying a shoe, turning off a lamp.
Ordinary, everyday activities are difficult
for those with distorted, twisted, painful joints.

Today, say a prayer for the person crippled with arthritis.

A Mother's Love

The mother of a girl with an eating disorder
is trying to make sense of this issue.
She is confused, shocked, worried, and ashamed.
She castigates herself for missing the signs
that all the professionals tell her
must have been so obvious in her daughter.
Apparently, she didn't see the signs
or realize what they meant.

Today she begins the process of getting her daughter help.
Today is the beginning
of what will be a very long struggle
for mother as well as daughter.

Include them both in your prayers today.

9/11 Survivor

We are all 9/11 survivors.
However, some were closer to the event than others.
They worked in the Pentagon and got out,
they worked in the World Trade Center and got out,
or they changed flights at the last minute.
Then there are those who were married to someone on the planes
or in the buildings,
the mother or the father who lost a child,
the child who lost a mother or father,
the sister without her brother.
They are the next of kin.
The survivor with the terrible heartache.
Think of one situation and say a prayer for healing and strength.

For Healing

Today say a prayer for a woman or girl who has been raped.
You may have passed her on the street today,
she may be in your office, or the clerk at the checkout counter,
or the voice on the end of the phone.
She could be next door or on the other side of the world.

Say a prayer for healing.

Swindled

Scam artists, con men, hustlers, frauds, fakes, and phonies
often target the elderly with their schemes.
How and what they do to swindle money,
obtain social security numbers,
account passwords, or entire savings from these victims
is not important. The victim is.
He might never recoup any of the money
and admitting that he turned over information,
wrote checks for a "good cause,"
and were blindsided by a smooth talker
is horribly embarrassing.
The victim often carries shame and self-loathing
from his lack of skepticism for the plan or investment
that sounded too good to be true.
For the victim of a scam,
who has lost money or his identity, or both,
along with the self-confidence to handle his own affairs,
say a prayer that he receives loving support from his family,
professional guidance to restore his finances,
and the ability to forgive himself.

Cutting Edge

Hard to know when it started,
all she knows is that it is hard to stop.
The girl who cuts herself
holds anger and pain and a razor.
There is guilt and shame and more cutting.
She needs her secret brought into the light.
Then she will need compassion, understanding,
and really good counseling.
She needs to find a release from her pain some other way.

She needs a prayer so that her healing can begin.

Baby's Breath

The babies in the neo-natal unit are the smallest souls among us
with the mightiest struggle for life.
Today, pray for one tiny baby,
the mom and dad who keep the vigil at her side,
the doctors and nurses who care for her needs and monitor her progress,
the pharmacist who prepares the medications in tiny dosages
for this tiny fighter.
Add your prayer to theirs so this little one becomes stronger each day.

Claire Coleman

Tiny Fighters

There are tiny babies who struggle to survive
in places where there are no neo-natal units,
no high-tech medical equipment,
no miraculous medicines.
They were born in desperately poor villages and towns,
or in some remote corner of the world,
yet the hopes and prayers of their families
are the same as every other loving parent:
just let her live,
just let him thrive.

Pray for those seemingly hopeless situations
and the sorrow
that settles on the family when nothing can be done.
Pray that governments and people put aside differences
and allow medical personnel and medicine
to cross borders and boundaries
for the sick and dying who need it so desperately.

Chapter 11

You Are in My Prayers

"I do not cease to give thanks for you
as I remember you in my prayers."
(Ephesians 1:16)

Claire Coleman

The Volunteer

There is no shortage of volunteer positions,
only a shortage of volunteers.
Still, people do come forward to serve at a soup kitchen,
deliver "Meals on Wheels,"
donate to a food pantry,
and arrive with blankets for the homeless on a cold night.

Say a prayer of thanks for someone who volunteers quietly,
but consistently,
and looks for no reward or recognition.

Knit One, Purl Two

She learned to knit from her grandmother,
who didn't believe in idle hands.
She keeps her hands busy making wool hats, gloves, and scarves.
She wraps each one in white tissue paper,
as if protecting an heirloom,
and offers a silent prayer
as she layers them in the shopping bag
to be delivered to a center for homeless families.
In her prayer she asks that each item finds its way
to someone in great need
and that it keeps that person warm during the winter.

Say a prayer of thanks today for the knitter nobody knows.

Do Over

Thousands of grandparents are raising their children's children.
Sometimes it is because the biological parents died,
or are very ill,
or mentally ill,
or battling an addiction,
or incarcerated,
or have abandoned the child.
The grandparents stepped in and stepped up
at a time when their bones were weary
from a lifetime of taking care of their own responsibilities.
Yet, they take on this new responsibility
because they value this innocent child
and are determined to see the child well fed, clothed,
educated, guided spiritually, and most of all, loved.

Say a prayer today for just one of those loving grandparents
who cooks meals, buys clothes, checks homework,
recites prayers, teaches manners,
and makes a child feel loved.

Smile Mobile

On the roads between the hills of Appalachia
a dentist drives his custom crafted eighteen-wheeler
to his next appointment.
He will park in one town for the day
so he and his staff can see patients.
This area leads the country in tooth decay,
young school children have cavities so deep and numerous,
their teeth are visibly corroding.
Some toddlers have rotten baby teeth
from drinking soda instead of milk.
The dentist-patient ratio is so high
that many people go for years without having their teeth checked.
Some people are known to pull out their own teeth with pliers.

Say a prayer of thanks for the people in the mobile dental office
for their creative solution to a serious problem
and for educating those they treat.

Drug Deals

There are pharmaceutical companies that research cures
for diseases most of us have never heard of and will never contract.
There are no US or European markets for any drugs they may develop,
but they devote time and money nonetheless.
Breakthroughs in medicine that target these often fatal illnesses
bring hope to thousands in underdeveloped nations.

Someone, someplace, approved research for drugs
that would never make money for the company or the stockholders.
He did it because it was the right thing to do.
Today in your prayers,
bless him and the men and women dedicated to the research.

Take Note

There are musicians who play very well,
not so well that they will ever be proclaimed as virtuosos.
But it doesn't matter.
For some, becoming famous is not a goal.
They want to teach music in high school or junior high.
They want to take on the marching band, the choral group,
the spring musical, a jazz group or the swing band.
They want to share their love of music,
open young minds to it, cultivate talent,
and hopefully, give each student some nugget of appreciation
for the mastery of great composers,
the variety of the world's music,
and the soul's innate connection to sound.

For those who bring music to the ears of children
and awaken a passion in a few lives along the way,
say a prayer of thanks for using their gifts and talents for others.

Having "Work" Done

Nose job, face-lift, eyebrow lift,
tummy tuck, nip and tuck,
liposuction, Botox, breast augmentation.
These words are associated with the cosmetic surgery
that eliminates wrinkles, drooping eyelids,
crepe-like skin on the neck,
love handles, flabby stomachs, or saddlebag thighs.
There are cosmetic surgeons who work on faces and bodies
that have been destroyed by burns, animal bites, knife attacks,
and other events that left victims with horrific facial injuries.
These doctors restore faces.
They restore what a person sees in a mirror,
what her loved ones see,
what the world sees.
They restore hope.

For specialists who rebuild something from nothing,
with knowledge, skill, and compassion,
a prayer of thanks for the devotion to the science and art of their field.

Day and Night

By day, he is a money manager with a major financial company,
handling multi-million dollar accounts
for well-heeled people who have amassed large fortunes.
But every Tuesday night, he is on the street with two other volunteers
handing out foil-wrapped sandwiches and cups of warm coffee
to people who have no home, sleep in a bus depot,
and carry all their pushcart possessions beside them.
No one in his office knows about the Tuesday nights
and those on the street don't know about his day job.

For the quiet volunteer,
putting his faith in action,
say a prayer of thanks,
especially on Tuesday nights.

The Way We Were

There are groups of people who dedicate their lives
to studying, unearthing, analyzing, charting, cataloging,
measuring, recording, debating, photographing, and writing
about history, artifacts, ancestors, wars, land and oceans,
the solar system, our government,
ancient governments, foreign governments,
ancient civilizations, social habits,
medical histories, antiques, biographies,
explorations, and dozens of other things
that are part of the material, physical, social, and metaphysical world.
These researchers, archeologists, historians, archivists,
philosophers, scientists, writers, geologists,
oceanographers, doctors, and many others
study, preserve, and make available information
about all that is and all that was.

Say a prayer for those who study the world
and the things and the people in it.
Their search for knowledge is insatiable, and their quest continues.

Miracles

The blind see,
the deaf hear,
the mute speak,
and the lame walk
because of men and women with creative, scientific minds
who embrace challenges and refuse to accept
that disabilities cannot be circumvented.
An idea, a sketch, a diagram, a prototype, a patient trial,
and finally, undeniable success—a product or procedure
that makes life more bearable for someone
who was forced to accept
a life-altering condition.

Say a prayer of thanks for researchers and scientists
who work to find a way to cheat the effects of a disability.

Get the Man

The lights go out,
or the furnace refuses to light,
or the toilet is overflowing,
or your basement is filling with water after a storm.
Sometimes there is nothing you can do about it,
so you make a call to the man.
The man with the tools, the know-how,
the pump, and a crew to help him.
When the job is finished, you are eternally grateful.
Plumbers, electricians, and sewer guys
don't have the most glamorous jobs
and don't make the most the money,
but when you need them,
it's nice to know a good one.

Just a simple prayer of thanks for those who come to our aid
in a time of need.

Old Masters

There are people who could never imagine
a workplace without sawdust at their feet.
Saws, chisels, planes, and levels are the tools of their trade.
With these tools in hand,
they craft and carve beautiful tables,
chairs, chests, moldings,
dollhouses, shelves, and desks.
They transform wood into art
with a touch
no machine can duplicate.
These masters preserve centuries-old woodworking traditions.

Say a prayer today that the creations of talented hands
are appreciated by others
and that woodworkers with extraordinary talent continue to create.

At Ease

The room is full of people who seem to all know each other
except, for one man,
who is obviously uncomfortable in this situation.
He tries to look busy,
fussing with the napkin around the bottom of his drink,
inspecting with "interest" an item on a table,
a painting on the wall,
but he still looks lost.
It is so apparent he needs a social lifesaver.
Then, someone approaches the man, talks to him, puts him at ease,
and introduces him to a larger group of people.

Say a prayer for the rescuer
who acts with compassion and without hesitation.

Hospice

Hospice means there is no going back to life as it used to be,
no getting better,
no pulling through,
no last ditch efforts that will be the saving grace,
no miracles.
Hospice also means adding grace, dignity, and kindness
when the opportunities for second chances narrow to none.
Sometimes, those entering hospice are so sick
as to be unaware of change in care,
but sometimes they are completely aware of this final step in their care,
and they must find peace with it.
Sometimes, it is the family who must stare the reality of hospice
squarely in the face.

For all those involved with one person
whose care is now in the hands of hospice,
say a prayer for a peaceful letting go and allowing for the will of God.

The Kindness of Strangers

Remember that man who picked up your wallet
when you dropped it at the dry cleaners?
Or the woman who handed you tissues
when your son had a bloody nose on the bus?
Or the Christmas shopper who held the last two copies of the video game
your kids wanted and then, seeing your disappointment,
handed you one?

Today the prayer you say should be for that person
who acted out of kindness and helped you out when you needed it.

Newborn

Consider all the babies born today and pray for just one of them.
The sick one or the healthy one.
The wanted or the unwanted.
The city hospital baby and the one born in a dirt floor hut.

May this baby thrive,
may he or she be loved and cared for tenderly as a gift from God.

Acknowledgements

While the idea for this book came to me rather effortlessly, the tasks of writing, revising, editing, proofreading, and those involved with publishing were anything but effortless.

In the beginning there was a small core group of friends who read the first drafts of *Special Intentions*. I could always count on Adele McHugh, Jean Marie Hofstetter, Stephanie Politi and Monica Battagliola for their feedback, their understanding of the project and their encouragement. In time I offered the manuscript to another friend, Julia Persinger, who in turn brought her husband, Joe into the reading ring. The Persingers' enthusiasm for *Special Intentions* has been unwavering.

Through Joe's kindness and his introduction, Amelia Grey became part of this circle of readers. In Amelia, I had more than just a reader; I had a wonderful resource, sounding board, coach and cheerleader. I can't thank her enough for providing me with clear direction and good advice.

Through the intercession of my sister, Ginny Needham-Doyle, I connected with Fr. James Martin, S. J., who became a font of information and advice. I took his words of wisdom to heart and revised the book's Introduction. He was right—it made a difference.

It was my good fortune to meet Martha Jewett and Evan Marshall, writers and agents with remarkable careers and talents. Their professional experience was a well from which I regularly drew. I am deeply grateful for their advice, guidance and friendship.

Dedicated writers with busy lives, Michelle Kobayshi, Jennifer Levine, Joanna Hinsey, Mary Silva and Aimee Bontreger, always found time to read and critique my work. I respect their knowledge of their craft and thank them for their support.

Mary Bushnell, Barbara Torres, Milvia Burns, Cathy Catalon, Karen Rodgers, and Rosemary Ellinwood are good friends who offered sympathetic ears and positive suggestions as I problem solved during the writing and editing process. I thank them for their invaluable friendship.

Knowing Frank Curtis and being able to reach out to him for legal advice is like having a lucky penny in your pocket. You don't always need it but it is comforting to know it is there. I thank him for his insights and advice.

All the credit for the outstanding artwork connected with *Special Intentions* belongs to Rosemary Tottoroto of PageOne Creative Group. Knowing Rosemary since college made working with her easy. There were things I didn't have to explain to her—she just knew them because she knew me. Ken Newbaker of PageOne Creative Group was my technological lifeline, and I appreciate his masterful work on the *Special Intentions* website. *(specialintentions.net)*

It has been a pleasure to partner with WestBow Press to produce *Special Intentions.* My thanks to all who guided me through the publishing process.

My sisters, Mitzi and Ginny, and my brother, John have been at my side through many journeys. This one is no exception. I thank them for their love and support.

My children, Matthew, Andrew and Maureen, are blessings for which I am ever grateful. They believed in the concept of *Special Intentions,* encouraged my efforts to write it and celebrated each milestone along the way with great joy.

My husband, Michael, is my staunchest advocate. His faith in me is ever-present, and that fact kept me afloat many days. He always gave me the time and space to write and loved me through it all. Thank you, with love, to Michael.

Special Intentions